DISCARD

THE COURSE SYLLABUS

THE COURSE SYLLABUS

A Learning-Centered Approach

Judith Grunert

Center for Instructional Development
Syracuse University

Foreword by Robert M. Diamond

ANKER PUBLISHING COMPANY, INC.
Bolton, MA

THE COURSE SYLLABUS
A Learning-Centered Approach

ISBN 1-882982-18-5

Composition by Deerfoot Studios.
Cover design by Deerfoot Studios.

Anker Publishing Company, Inc.
176 Ballville Road
P. O. Box 249
Bolton, MA 01740-0249

ABOUT THE AUTHOR

Judith Grunert's current research is concerned with how faculty across disciplines in higher education approach their research. She is presently at the Syracuse University Center for Instructional Development where she works with faculty in various disciplines to improve learning. Grunert's interests center on the ways that instructors in higher education can help students to become the agents of their own education. She draws upon her experience as a member of the School of Art faculty, College of Visual and Performing Arts, Syracuse University, and as a Lilly Endowment Fellow, when she developed curricular and instructional materials that would help students assume increasing responsibility over planning, implementing, and evaluating their learning experiences.

Grunert has coordinated and contributed to the design and development of national educational projects for higher education, government, and not-for-profit organizations. She exhibits her sculpture and drawings at museums and galleries.

CONTENTS

FOREWORD

A transformation is underway in American higher education, shifting the focus away from what faculty members teach to what students learn—from what Robert Barr and John Tagg (1995) have called the *instructional paradigm* to what they call the *learning paradigm*. This new perspective calls for a shift in the faculty role from disseminator of knowledge to facilitator of learning. The shift calls for changes in how we think about the courses we teach, how we design students' learning experiences, and how we articulate our expectations of our students and ourselves.

Technology, changing demographics, and new ways of thinking about the nature of knowledge in the Information Age have prompted many changes in approaches to teaching on college and university campuses. In addition, new opportunities available through the Internet and e-mail, as well as internships and extended classroom activities have affected significantly the nature of what and how we teach. The traditional syllabus was never developed to help students understand their expanding role in the learning enterprise. In order to understand the expectations faculty have of them and the plans that have been established for the learning experience, students need more comprehensive information than the traditional syllabus provides. The learning-centered syllabus addresses student learning and responds to the question: What do students need to know in order to derive maximum benefit from this educational experience?

Many faculty have already gone far beyond the one- or two-page traditional syllabus. John Lough (1997), in a study of Carnegie Professor of the Year award-winning faculty, found important similarities in syllabi designed by these exemplary teachers. Most obvious was the detailed precision of the syllabi. Each contained clearly stated course objectives; a day-by-day schedule identifying specific reading assignments and due dates; and clear statements regarding make-up dates, attendance, and grading standards. They also provided students with the times when the professor would be available in the office, by e-mail, and by phone at home. Lough observed, "One gets the very clear impression that the Carnegie award winners have extraordinary expectations for their own behavior in and out of the classroom. Perhaps it is not so surprising, therefore, that these professors might impose some of these same standards on the students with whom they share so much." These high standards are manifest by what they do in the classroom and also by what they say in their syllabi.

In order to begin that communication process, an effective learning-centered syllabus should accomplish certain basic goals:

- Define students' responsibilities
- Define instructor's role and responsibility to students
- Provide a clear statement of intended goals and student outcomes
- Establish standards and procedures for evaluation
- Acquaint students with course logistics (a particularly important element as we include more group work and out of class experiences)
- Establish a pattern of communication between instructor and students
- Include difficult to obtain materials such as readings, complex charts, and graphs

The syllabus is an important product; equally important and useful is the process of developing a comprehensive student syllabus—a reflective exercise that leads to course improvement. In the process of thinking through questions of course content, activities, and practices such as assessment and grading, you will be confronted with questions of consistency and practicality as well as questions about how well what you do in your course supports the goals that you have for student learning. Such considerations will lead to a more carefully designed course—and one that consistently focuses on your students and their learning.

Focusing on learning rather than teaching requires a shift from an overview of what you as the instructor will cover to consideration of what your students need in order to be successful learners. This change in focus can also affect the student's role in your course. Accepting responsibility for their own learning can be difficult for students who have been educated, as most have, as passive listeners. This change in role may be particularly difficult for some international students who come from cultures in which asking questions of the professor is openly discouraged and perceived as unacceptable student behavior.

Your syllabus is your first opportunity to introduce the learning-centered paradigm to your students and to describe for them the role and responsibilities they will have in your class. You can ease this transition for your students by communicating in a comprehensive manner what the expectations are for your course. A carefully developed and effectively used syllabus can actively support their learning and success. This practical guide has been prepared to assist you in developing such a syllabus.

Robert M. Diamond
Assistant Vice Chancellor
Center for Instructional Development
Syracuse University

PREFACE

Myriad challenges face American colleges and universities today, among them serving an increasingly diverse student population and responding to the demands of an information society that is transforming the way we live and work. A renewed focus on student learning is one way of meeting those challenges. For instructors in higher education, this will involve rethinking learning goals and teaching priorities in an effort to assure active, purposeful, and effective learning.

This guide frames the process of developing a comprehensive student syllabus as a reflective exercise that leads to course improvement. Composing a syllabus that is centered on student learning is a challenging undertaking that requires substantial reflection and analysis. A learning-centered syllabus requires that you shift from what you, the instructor, are going to cover in your course to a concern for what information and tools you can provide for your students to promote learning and intellectual development.

Your syllabus represents a significant point of interaction, often the first, between you and your students. If thoughtfully prepared, your syllabus will demonstrate the interplay of your understanding of students' needs and interests; your beliefs and assumptions about the nature of learning and education; and your values and interests concerning course content and structure. If carefully designed, your syllabus will provide your students with essential information and resources that can help them to become effective learners by actively shaping their own learning. It will minimize misunderstandings by providing you and your students with a common plan and reference.

ORGANIZATION

Part I of this book reflects on the implications of a focus on learning for you and your students, and guides you to the discovery of fresh insights and new ways to develop a course syllabus. Included are sections on planning a learning-centered syllabus, composing it to serve a number of functions, and using your syllabus as learning tool throughout your course. The discussions in each section include brief consideration of computer technology related to syllabus form, function, and use.

Part II offers some helpful examples drawn from existing course syllabi and course manuals. These examples were not necessarily developed within a framework of learning-centeredness, yet each contributes something to this perspective.

Part III includes an annotated list of suggested readings that you should find useful for further exploration of issues raised in this guide. The topics include general teaching, active learning, cooperative learning, critical thinking, assessment, student differences, course and curriculum design, and finally, references on developing an annotated teaching portfolio that you can use to document innovations and improvements in your teaching.

BENEFITS TO INSTRUCTORS

As the instructor responsible for teaching a course, you are usually responsible for developing course materials, starting with a course syllabus. This book will help you. In the process of thinking through how well what you do in your course will support the goals that you have set for student learning, you will confront issues of consistency and practicality among your rationale, course content, student activities, and your assessment and grading practices. These considerations will lead to a more carefully designed course, one that consistently focuses on your students and their learning.

Your learning-centered syllabus can help to reinforce your expectations for the roles that you expect students to take in your course. You will be prepared both to help those students who may not be familiar or comfortable with active and collaborative learning approaches, and to overcome their concerns by providing concrete descriptions of tools and procedures that will support these approaches.

While this guide was developed with college and university instructors in mind, it should also be useful to others:

- Faculty mentors of junior faculty, new faculty, and TAs

- Department chairs, program directors, and deans

- Administrators of academic affairs

- Faculty development specialists

- Students of educational practice

- Other post-secondary educators

Transforming your courses into the kinds of educational environments where students share responsibility for shaping their learning is an evolving process, for you as well as for your students. Developing a learning-centered syllabus can be a stimulus to you and also to your colleagues in clarifying curricular goals and instructional priorities and for conversations about how to promote learning.

Judith Grunert
Center for Instructional Development
Syracuse University

ACKNOWLEDGMENTS

This guide is based on an original concept by Cathy A. Rogers and Robert E. Burnett in *Student Manuals: Their Rationale and Design* (1980), produced and copyrighted by the Center for Instructional Development (CID), Syracuse University.

All of the staff at CID deserve thanks for their support during the many revisions of this guide. I want to thank in particular, Bob Diamond, Bron Adam, and Ruth Stein whose thoughtful readings and generous criticisms helped me to prune an unwieldy amount of material and develop a useful structure. Abby Kasowitz helped with analysis, selection, and editing of the examples in an early draft, and provided insights about evaluation and grading. Rob Pusch reviewed sections on computer technology. Julie Mills formatted the text and layout of successive drafts. Pam Leighton provided helpful information about securing copyright permissions, and she and Jishnu Shankar printed earlier review versions of the guide. Questions from Phil Doughty and Chuck Spuches on the developing versions pushed me to be more clear.

Most of the examples used in this guide were drawn from student manuals produced and copyrighted by the Center for Instructional Development at Syracuse University. A special thanks goes to those faculty and other friends of CID who allowed me to use examples from their course syllabi and course manuals. Their names are included in the references.

Finally, I want to thank Jim and Susan Anker for the insightful suggestions that they made in response to early drafts. Those suggestions prompted the transformation of the guide into its present form.

Part I
Focus on Learning

Colleges and universities across the United States are making a fresh commitment to student learning. Many would argue that learning has always been central in their institutions; however, there is an important difference in what is happening now. Students from underrepresented racial, ethnic, and linguistic backgrounds; women; and older adults are questioning an educational perspective that has been tuned to predominantly middle class European-American male experiences (Wlodkowski & Ginsberg, 1995). Along with the recognition of multiple perspectives comes a responsibility that colleges and universities are trying to meet through a renewed focus on students and how they learn. As an instructor, placing your students' learning and development as a priority means that you must consider their varied educational needs, interests, and purposes as you determine the content and structure of your course.

Your students live and work in a world where the quality and quantity of information changes rapidly, and what counts as knowledge alters with time and context. Knowledge is increasingly important and is expanding exponentially. The effects of information technology and communications technology have produced profound changes in the way we live and work. Students will need to recognize when information is required, know how to locate and retrieve information, and how to analyze and criticize that information so that it becomes useful knowledge (ALA, 1989, in Bergquist & Sharpe, 1996).

You need only consider the situations students will face after graduation to appreciate the importance of a focus on learning for your course and your syllabus. Our contemporary lives have intensified our need to know how to learn, both alone and in collaboration with others. On leaving school, your students will encounter complex problems on a daily basis and will come to recognize that contradiction and change are natural states of affairs. Faced

1

with multiple and often conflicting perspectives, they will continually be forced to break out of old thought patterns, to think in new ways. They will have to make commitments in situations devoid of clear rules, norms, and criteria (Bergquist & Sharpe, 1996).

PREPARING STUDENTS

Preparing your students for the purposeful and effective lifelong learning that these conditions require has strong implications for course content, structure, and for the materials and strategies you use to promote learning. Students will require more carefully thought out information and well-honed tools in order to prepare them for an expanded role in learning.

It is important that college and university students learn how to actively construct, apply, assess, and extend their knowledge in a sustained, ongoing process (Brown, 1993). At one time, college teaching was typified by presenting information through authoritative lectures and readings, testing students on their knowledge, and assigning grades. Recent research on students' academic success, intellectual development, theories of cognitive development and learning demonstrates the effectiveness of teaching modes that emphasize active learning, collaborative activities, and critical and creative intellectual inquiry (Pascarella & Terenzini, 1991). Help is available through rapidly growing bodies of literature that offer ways to prevent discrimination and affirm students' intellectual and cultural diversity in classrooms.

Learning strategists present numerous options for diversifying approaches to teaching and for reexamining the limited ways in which we define intelligence. Evaluation and assessment scholars are leading a revolution to change narrow and exclusive assessment standards and practices. Systems theorists support and model ways to locate dysfunction within institutional practices rather than within human beings (Wlodkowski & Ginsberg, 1995).

SETTING A FRAMEWORK FOR KNOWLEDGE

Learning is an active, constructive, contextual process; new knowledge is acquired in relation to previous knowledge; information becomes meaningful when it is presented and acquired in some type of framework. From a learning-centered perspective, your task as instructor is to interact with students in ways that enable them to acquire new information, practice new skills, reconfigure what they already know, and know what they have learned (Davis, 1993a).

A learning-centered approach has subtle but profound implications for you as a teacher. It asks that you think carefully about your teaching philosophy, what it means to be an educated person in your discipline or field, how your course relates to disciplinary and interdisciplinary programs of study, and your intentions and purposes for producing and assessing learning. It asks that you think through the implications of your preferred teaching style, the choices you make about teaching strategies, forms of assessment, and the ways that students' diverse needs, interests, and purposes can influence those choices.

ENCOURAGING RESPONSIBILITY FOR LEARNING

A learning-centered approach asks to what extent you can support and challenge students to assume increasing responsibility for actively shaping their learning—in your course and in the future. As you prepare a syllabus to promote student learning, consider the balance between instructor leadership and student initiative in all of your course activities and ask yourself to what extent students are involved in the following:

- Participating in planning all phases of their individual learning process

- Clarifying their own goals for the course

- Monitoring and assessing their own progress

- Establishing criteria for judging their own performance, within the educational intentions of the course (including any limitations imposed by certification or licensing), the constraints of time, and respect for the needs of other students

DEVELOPING A LEARNING-CENTERED SYLLABUS

A learning-centered approach to college education asks you to consider how each and every aspect of your course can most effectively support student learning. How, then, can you use your syllabus to promote your students' engagement with subject matter and their intellectual development?

Your syllabus can be an important point of interaction between you and your students, both in and out of class. The traditional syllabus is primarily a source of information for your students. While including basic information, the learning-centered syllabus can be an important learning tool that will reinforce the intentions, roles, attitudes, and strategies that you will use to promote active, purposeful, effective learning.

The sections in this first part of the book will help you to plan, compose, and use a learning-centered syllabus.

PLANNING YOUR LEARNING-CENTERED SYLLABUS: AN OVERVIEW OF THE PROCESS

Planning a learning-centered syllabus is an important stage in the process of crafting educational experiences for your students. The process first requires a well-developed rationale concerning your personal beliefs and assumptions about the nature of learning and how it is promoted and produced. It requires next that you establish what skills, knowledge, and attitudes you believe are of most worth, how they can be built into your course, and how they will be appropriately assessed. It requires that you create a learning environment for your students using teaching and learning strategies that are consistent with those beliefs. And finally, it requires that you compose a syllabus that will communicate your expectations and intentions to your students.

Course development is beyond the scope of this guide, but this section will provide a brief overview of the process that leads to composing your syllabus. The next sections, Composing a Learning-Centered Syllabus, and Using a Learning-Centered Syllabus offer suggestions for ways to communicate these important concepts to your students. Part II provides examples that faculty have developed for use in course syllabi and course manuals that contribute to a learning-centered perspective. An annotated bibliography is provided at the end of the guide to help with many of the issues raised here.

PLANNING YOUR SYLLABUS

- Develop a well-grounded rationale for your course
- Decide what you want students to be able to do as a result of taking your course, and how their work will be appropriately assessed
- Define and delimit course content
- Structure your students' active involvement in learning
- Identify and develop resources
- Compose your syllabus with a focus on student learning

DEVELOP A WELL-GROUNDED RATIONALE FOR YOUR COURSE

The composition of your syllabus is integrally tied to your rationale for the design of your course. All aspects of your course are influenced by the sometimes taken for granted beliefs and implicit assumptions that frame how you think about and practice the educational process. A well-grounded rationale for your practice, "a set of critically examined core assumptions about why you do what you do in the way that you do it" (Shulman & Hutchings, 1994) will help you to make decisions about what to include in your syllabus. Shulman and Hutchings suggest that such reflection on teaching is an act of scholarship. The questions they suggest to guide reflection on teaching are summarized in Figure 1.

Wlodkowski and Ginsberg (1995) suggest further that as you develop your syllabus you check it for bias. Scan the entire syllabus for the norms it reflects and think about how you might remodel your course and your syllabus to be more intellectually and culturally responsive. Changes you make in your syllabus can profoundly affect the learning process and clarify your expectations of how the knowledge of the course is constructed.

FIGURE 1

SCHOLARLY REFLECTION ABOUT TEACHING

Shulman and Hutchings (1994) suggest that you think about the ways your course and syllabus represent acts of scholarship. Adopt a stance of inquiry toward your practice, seeing your ideas and practices in constant formation and always in need of further investigation. Before composing the syllabus, engage in scholarly reflection about your teaching.

- Every course we craft is a lens into our fields and our personal conceptions of those disciplines. Give careful thought to the shape and content of your course. How does the course begin? Why does it begin where it does? (What is the thesis of the argument?) What do you and your students do as the course unfolds? What do you lecture about or lead discussions around? What are the key assignments or student evaluations? (What are the main points of the argument? What are the key bodies of evidence?) How does it end? Why does it end as it does? (Most scholarly arguments carry the intention to persuade.) What do you want to persuade your students to believe? Or question? Or do you want them to develop new appetites or dispositions?

- Are there distinctly different ways to organize your course—ways that reflect quite different perspectives on your discipline or field? Do you focus on particular topics while other colleagues might make other choices? Why?

- In what ways does your course teach students how scholars work in your field—the methods, procedures, and values which shape how knowledge claims are made and adjudicated? How does it open doors to the critical dialogues and key arguments scholars are engaged in at the cutting edge of your field?

- How does your course connect with other courses in your own or other fields? To what extent does your course lay a foundation for others that follow it? Or build on what students have learned in other courses? Or challenge and contradict what students are learning in your own or other disciplines? How does your course fit within a larger conception of curriculum, program, and teaching?

- What do you expect students to find particularly fascinating about your course? Where will they encounter the greatest difficulties of either understanding or motivation? How does the content of your course connect to matters your students already understand or have experienced? Where will it seem most alien? How do you address these common student responses in your course? How has the course evolved over time in response to them?

- Try playing with some metaphors for characterizing your course and its place in the larger curriculum or in the broader intellectual and moral intellectual lives of your students. Is your course like a journey, a parable, a football game, a museum, a romance, a concerto, an Aristotelian tragedy, an obstacle course, one or all or some of the above? How does your metaphor(s) illuminate key aspects of your course?

Decide on Desired Outcomes and Assessment Measures

Plan your course with process, content, and product goals in mind. For example, in addition to the conceptual knowledge and technical skills of a discipline or field, your students will need other tools for living and working effectively in society. Students should be able to do the following:

- Initiate, understand, assess, and assume responsibility for their own ongoing learning process

- Access and use resources effectively
- Work alone and collaborate with others
- Resolve dilemmas emerging from complex situations
- Think and communicate effectively using appropriate means such as writing, speaking and listening, numbers, graphics, digital, 3D form, or performance
- Clarify personal values, purposes, and goals
- Understand and respect differences

Whenever you formulate learning goals you should simultaneously address assessment procedures. According to Wlodkowski and Ginsberg (1995), assessment is a procedure for gathering information about the learning process that uses multiple indicators and sources of evidence. Become more conscious of your assessment philosophy and develop an understanding of how your approach to assessment fits with your beliefs about teaching and learning. Use multiple measures to avoid limiting judgments to one or two high stakes testing occasions or one particular kind of assessment task. They recommend the following norms for developing an assessment philosophy:

- The assessment process is connected to the learners' world, frames of reference, and values.

- Demonstration of learning includes multiple ways to represent knowledge and skills and allows for attainment of outcomes at different points in time.

- Self-assessment is essential to the overall assessment process.

As they accept increasing responsibility for their learning, students must develop the tools for self-assessment that will help them improve upon and internalize criteria for monitoring and judging their own performance. You can establish creative forms of evaluation, beyond paper and pencil tests, with clearly stated standards and criteria, that will provide useful, ongoing, and final information for both you and your students (Davis, 1993b). For example, product assessment (essays, stories, research reports, writing portfolios, projects, etc.), performance assessments (music, dance, dramatic performance, science lab demonstrations, debates, experiments, action research, etc.), and process-focused assessment (oral questioning, interviews, learning logs, process folios, journals, observation, etc.) (Wlodkowski & Ginsberg,

1995). It is important that your assessment and grading strategies are consistent with your rationale.

If your evaluation criteria are clearly understood and seem fair to your students, the students can more easily evaluate their own work and be more assured about the results. When students participate in determining the criteria by which work will be judged and then play a role in assessing their work (or the work of other students) against those criteria, their personal sense of responsibility for learning is more apparent. This is an important learning experience in itself. "Students can derive immense intellectual benefits from considering what makes an essay well written, a problem solution creative, an example conceptually clear" (Wlodkowski & Ginsberg, 1995).

DEFINE AND DELIMIT COURSE CONTENT

Be clear about what is most worth knowing. The use of active learning may limit the amount of content you can cover in a course, but much of the conceptual material many instructors now cover is poorly learned and soon forgotten. Choose the outcomes you value most. Discipline yourself to prune away forgettable and forgotten content and focus on the more important knowledge, skills, and values (Davis,1993a). One way of thinking about content is to place it in three categories: content that all students will be required to know, content that you will make available to support individual student inquiry or projects, and content that might only be of interest to a student who wants to specialize in this area. Excessive emphasis on transmission of large quantities of information infringes on the time students need to transform information into useful knowledge (Kurfiss, 1988). Develop a conceptual framework (theory, theme, controversial issue) which will support major ideas and topics. If critical thinking is one of your goals for your students, what questions, issues, and problems can frame your course? (Davis,1993a). A summary of principles that foster critical thinking has been provided in Figure 2.

STRUCTURE YOUR STUDENTS'
ACTIVE INVOLVEMENT IN LEARNING

Decide what topics are appropriate to what types of student activities and assignments. Will your course topics tend toward a content or a process orientation? Which activities and types of products can involve students in sustained intensive work, both independently and with one another? What activities will help students to learn the tools of the discipline or field? How can you develop a challenging and supportive course climate that builds student effectiveness, specifically teaches interpersonal and collaborative skills, and develops the capacity for lifelong learning? What strategies will you use to shape basic skills and procedures, present information, guide inquiry, monitor individual and group activities, and support and challenge critical reflection?

J. R. Davis (1993) advocates an eclectic approach, using teaching and learning strategies for their strengths to achieve different purposes. General instructional strategies include training and coaching, lecturing and explaining, inquiry and discovery, groups and teams, experience and reflection. To be effective, Davis emphasizes that the strategies you choose must fit with the outcomes you hope to achieve—some delineation of goals and possibilities for instruction. Implementing a strategy involves making the strategy work for the subject; the setting; and the varied capacities, knowledge, skills, and experiences of these students.

FIGURE 2

PRINCIPLES FOR DESIGNING A COURSE THAT FOSTERS CRITICAL THINKING

A good critical thinking course presents students with "problems, questions, and issues" that make a course "assignment centered rather than text or lecture centered" and holds students responsible for "formulating their solutions in writing or other appropriate means. Attention is also given to the design of problems at appropriate levels of difficulty, to the developmental needs of students, and to the importance of making expectations and criteria clear. In each case, the instructor establishes an agenda that includes learning to think about subject matter. Students are active, involved, consulting and arguing with each other, and responsible for their own learning" (Bean, 1996; Kurfiss, 1988).

From her examination of a wide number of courses, Kurfiss (1988) has derived eight principles for designing a disciplinary course that supports critical thinking:

1) Critical thinking is a learnable skill; the instructor and peers are resources in developing critical thinking skills.

2) Problems, questions, or issues are the point of entry into the subject and a source of motivation for sustained inquiry.

3) Successful courses balance the challenge to think critically with support tailored to students' developmental needs.

4) Courses are assignment centered rather than text and lecture centered. Goals, methods, and evaluation emphasize using content rather than simply acquiring it.

5) Students are required to formulate their ideas in writing or other appropriate means.

6) Students collaborate to learn and to stretch their thinking, for example, in pair problem solving and small group work.

7) Courses that teach problem solving skills nurture students' metacognitive abilities.

8) The developmental needs of students are acknowledged and used as information in the design of the course. Teachers in these courses make standards explicit and then help students learn how to achieve them.

IDENTIFY/ASSEMBLE RESOURCES
REQUIRED FOR ACTIVE LEARNING

Active thinkers, those engaged in speaking and listening, reading, writing, and reflecting about a topic of interest, assemble a rich array of resources (people, materials, and strategies) to facilitate their creative intellectual activity, both alone and in collaboration with others. You can specify a core or central body of information and "seed the environment" with other ideas and concepts that you value (Brown, 1993). Consider ways to include alternate and conflicting perspectives through lectures and panel presentations, demonstrations, books, and readings. Also consider films, videos, maps, libraries, museums, theaters, studios, labs, data bases, sites on the Internet, and other materials which students can appropriate and transform through personal interpretation.

You can challenge students to search for further information or new, even contradictory, points of view that may be relevant to the issues, questions, and problems or that will support individual student's "self-initiated tangents" (Brown, 1993) and special projects.

Request Permission to Use Copyrighted Materials

When assembling your course readings and other course materials, take care to obtain the necessary permission from the copyright owner before duplicating articles, graphics, or other materials that you want to include. Fair use does not allow for extensive or repeated copying. Securing copyright permissions can be a time-consuming and sometimes costly process.

Authors are protected by federal statute against unauthorized use of their unpublished manuscripts. Under the Copyright Act of 1976 (Title 17 of the *United States Code*), an unpublished work is copyrighted from the moment it is fixed in tangible form—for example, typed on a page. Copyright protection is "an incident of the process of authorship" (US Copyright Office, 1981). Until the author formally transfers copyright, the author owns the copyright on an unpublished manuscript, and all exclusive rights due the owner of a copyright of a published work are also due the author of an unpublished work. To ensure copyright protection, include the copyright notice on all published works. The notice need not appear on unpublished materials. Registration of copyright provides a public record and is usually a prerequisite for legal action.

To request permission to reprint, you must first contact the holder of the copyright. When the holder is a publishing house, contact its copyright department to find out what is required. Some publishers use a copyright clearing house such as the *Copyright Clearance Center*. Typically you will need to provide author, title, ISBN #, publisher, chapter/article, # copies, # pages, college/university, course title, instructor, and a copy of what you are requesting permission to use. You can mail or fax a letter to the publisher or the clearing house providing this information. Getting permission to reprint typically takes six to eight weeks, so plan to begin the process at least two months before printing is scheduled. Some clearing houses such as *Copyright Clearance Center* (www.copyright.com) are now on-line.\

MOVING FROM PLANNING TO COMPOSING

Once you know why you do what you do, what your significant content and process goals are for your course, and how you will provide opportunities for active, productive thinking about significant questions, issues, and problems in your field, and opportunities to assess learning, a question remains. How will you introduce these ideas to your students? The next section discusses some possible functions for your syllabus.

Composing a Learning-Centered Syllabus

In higher education, every course, every group of students, and every instructor is unique, and their particular combination of features should determine the exact content and form of the syllabus. Your syllabus can be a brief document or an extended text affording a view of your course and its significance. Regardless of your focus—traditional or learning-centered— some basic information should be included.

Syllabus Content

Students generally want to know about the purpose of the course; nature of class sessions; level of preparation or background necessary to succeed; required textbooks, readings, and supplies; topics that will be covered; number and type of tests and assignments; grading system used; and policies pertaining to attendance, late work, and make-up work (Davis, 1993a). If you are preparing a syllabus for the first time, you can begin with these features.

A learning-centered approach to composing a syllabus incorporates these features but goes further, focusing on the value of your syllabus as a learning tool in your course. It can convey the logic and organization of the course and clarify instructional priorities, providing a common plan and reference. Your syllabus can clarify the mutual responsibilities of both you and your students in successfully meeting course goals. It can provide students with a way to assess your whole course plan, its rationale, content, activities, policies, and scheduling in order to achieve some personal control over their learning process.

A learning-centered syllabus includes more rather than less information. It provides students with the resources of a course manual, with each component crafted to promote student learning.

Syllabus Form

When you lay out your syllabus, remember that it is a reference document that is often read piecemeal. Instructors handle this in different ways: with emphatic headings, mechanical breaks, or other spatial arrangements that clearly demarcate material and make the readings, grading policy, schedule, etc., easy for students to locate (Project Advance, 1995).

Longer versions of a syllabus should have three-hole punched pages which can be inserted in a three-ring binder. Students can then include their own notes and personal resources in one location.

SYLLABUS ON-LINE

Faculty who have placed the syllabus on a local server or Web home page welcome the opportunity to take advantage of the hypertext environment, to make changes and additions readily, and to create links to other resources for their students. Most still require students to have a hard copy for common reference in the classroom. They view the syllabus as both a dynamic learning tool and a contract that they review carefully on the first day of class and return to frequently throughout the course.

Before placing course material on-line, it is important to take a realistic look at your computing environment (Polyson, Saltzberg, & Goodwin-Jones, 1996). Know how students will be accessing your course materials: from on-campus computer networks, including labs, classrooms, and dorms; or from an off-site location. This is important because it affects connection speed. Be prepared to tell your students how to access your materials. For example, identify which campus labs have Internet access and the necessary software, provide information about campus SLIP/PPP dial-in service, and explain how to obtain service through a commercial Internet service provider.

Identify computer hardware and software requirements (such as a Web browser) for your students before you design your on-line course materials. Along with knowledge about student access, hardware and software will affect how students can use these materials. Faster connection speeds of campus networks allow for the use of video clips and elaborate visual images that will be problematic for those using slower dial-in services. Sound clips will only be useful to students who use computers capable of audio playback.

Students' technological competence will vary. Investigate the technical support that will be available to your students both on and off campus in anticipation of the inevitable technical problems that will need to be resolved.

All Web documents are created using HTML (hypertext mark-up language) the basic programming language of the Web. Many new software products have been developed which make the creation of HTML documents almost as easy as using standard word processing software if you are limiting your syllabus to text only. Microsoft and WordPerfect have HTML add-ins to their word processors. Those wishing to explore more sophisticated high-end technology can use Java, JavaScript, and CGI to add interactivity or animation.

Once you've created your Web pages, you will need to work with your college or university computing staff to move your Web pages to the institution's Web server (unless you or your department runs a Web server). If you wish to restrict access only to students in your class, you will need to work with your Web server administrator to create log-ins and passwords for each student.

Instructors who put their course syllabi on-line can link them to resources throughout the world. The syllabus can be easily updated as new resources become available and can provide students with a current picture of course requirements. Homework assignments can be directly linked on-line to the class schedule.

Syllabus Functions

Your syllabus can serve a wide variety of functions that will support and challenge students as they engage in their educational activities.

1) Establishes an Early Point of Contact and Connection Between Student and Instructor

Research has shown that students want more frequent interaction with faculty. You can begin to communicate your availability by including basic information such as your name, address, telephone number, e-mail address, office hours, how to arrange for a conference. [See Examples, Part II] You can also include a page soliciting biographical information (also address, phone #, e-mail, etc.) that will help you to learn students' names, their interests, and why they are in the course. To encourage interaction with other students in the course, you might use this information to develop a student roster (including name, address, phone #, e-mail, etc.) that is particularly useful for group work and work time out of class. You can include similar information about other important student contacts, such as TAs, technicians, main office staff, and librarians, when appropriate. This contact information will be useful in case plans change during the course of the term or semester.

2) Helps Set the Tone for Your Course

Your syllabus communicates much about your attitudes toward students and learning. The way in which you communicate your views helps students to understand whether your class will be conducted in a formal or informal manner. Communicating an openness to questions, concerns, and dialogue begins with the syllabus.

3) Describes Your Beliefs About Educational Purposes

You can explain whether your course has a product or a process orientation and how that determines your expectations of students. Explain how you have set your agenda for the course, how the course structure reinforces goals and objectives, how the activities and assignments will help them to meet both product and process goals. You may describe learning strategies and techniques you will use and your rationale for using them. You can make explicit how your criteria and standards for both their work process and products are aligned with course goals.

4) Acquaints Students with the Logistics of the Course

Courses vary in terms of the days classes meet, the instructors for each class, and the type of sessions which occur (i.e., guest lecturers, teamwork sessions, simulations, films, etc.). Your syllabus can detail this information so that students will know what to expect and can be prepared for each class meeting. Providing students with a course calendar helps them to plan their work. Noting holidays and any days on which class will be canceled or rescheduled allows students to plan ahead and prevents misunderstandings. It also shows that you respect the value of students' time. [See Examples, Part II]

5) Contains Collected Handouts

Faculty often distribute handouts as they become appropriate to the topics covered. Often students put them into whatever notebook is at hand and then find it difficult to retrieve them. By planning your course, preparing the necessary handouts, and including them in your syllabus, you help students, among other things, to keep all course material together and accessible. These items, among other things, might include biographical information forms, detailed information on assignments, various evaluation forms, or diagrams and other visual representations.

6) Defines Student Responsibilities for Successful Course Work

Your syllabus can help students to achieve some personal control over their learning, to plan their semester, and to manage their time effectively. If your students have a clear idea of *what* they are expected to accomplish, *when*, and even *why*, they will be more likely to finish assignments within a reasonable time and be appropriately prepared for classes and exams.

7) Describes Active Learning

Students often conceive of learning as the acquisition of correct information, but they may not know what it means to take an active role in the process, beyond rote memorization and recall. You can include a description of your expectations for student initiative in your syllabus. If critical thinking, problem solving, and inquiry are part of your course, it is helpful to tell students that they will be asked to consider multiple viewpoints and conflicting values and to imagine, analyze, and evaluate alternate positions on issues or solutions to problems.

It is also important to describe what students can expect from you in your role as teacher: content expert, formal authority, socializing agent, facilitator, role model, experienced learner, resource consultant, coach, counselor.

8) Helps Students to Assess Their Readiness for Your Course

What are the prerequisites for your course? In addition to specific course prerequisites, students should be given some idea about what they should already know and what skills they should already have before taking your course so they can realistically assess their readiness. Your syllabus can provide information about the challenges students will face, the assumed skill level, the skills they will build upon, and the skills they will learn during your course. You may also include information about institutional or other sources for academic support. Some faculty include self-assessment tools and learning contracts to assist students with this process.

9) Sets the Course in a Broader Context for Learning

Your syllabus can provide a perspective that allows students to see instructors in your discipline as active and experienced learners engaged in inquiry in their professional fields or disciplines. Many students are unaware that their instructors are involved in research and creative professional activity beyond the classroom, that they are not simply transmitters of knowledge and skills.

You can encourage your students to approach the learning situation as apprentice learners in a community of scholars. You can help them to see you and other faculty as experienced active learners who can provide expert guidance about general and specialized knowledge of content and practice in your field.

Your syllabus can provide information that shows students how your course fits within the discipline or profession, the general program of study, and their own educational plans. You can make students aware that every discipline or field has its unique way of knowing. You can encourage students to approach the field actively as ethnographic fieldworkers who want to understand the social and intellectual practices of the field. Assure them that you will guide them while they learn how to use the characteristic tools and modes of inquiry, patterns of explanation, discourse practices, and the types of artifacts that are valued and produced in their field.

10) Provides a Conceptual Framework

Your syllabus can support major ideas, topics, and factual information. Include in it questions or issues for students to think about that range from major issues or key questions in the discipline to the meaning of a significant passage in a course reading (Bean, 1996). Such a framework will help students organize information and focus their learning.

11) Describes Available Learning Resources

You can list campus resources such as libraries, reserve desks, reading rooms, laboratories, computer clusters, and studios that students may use (including their locations, availability, and policies) as well as any information concerning the location and use of aids such as tape recordings, copy services, CD ROMs or videos. You may also note the locations of specific books, videos, and sites on computer networks. [See Examples, Part II]

12) Communicates the Role of Technology in the Course

Computers and computer networks have increased our ability to access information and communicate with each other. Computers are working tools that students use for their own learning: to enhance their thinking; plan and revise learning goals; monitor and reflect on their progress; set up and access their own personal knowledge files; share a common database; build their own database; use a spreadsheet; run statistical software; keep a journal; write, illustrate, and revise texts; and build up a portfolio. You can use computers as a resource tool to provide direct instruction of new content, tutorials, and interactive simulations; to model extremely small or large phenomena (Brown, 1993; Davis, 1993a).

E-mail is a practical way to interact with your students. Assignments, comments on their work, important class information, and questions to you and to other students, and extended classroom discussions are all possible uses and allow documents to be prepared, sent, received, and read by the recipient at convenient times.

Institutions, individual faculty, and students are creating their own home pages on the World Wide Web or using information servers to share course materials on-line, such as your learning-centered syllabus, reading lists, lecture outlines or notes, collaborative software, and other course information. When you use servers and the World Wide Web, you can control the information you want to access by navigating through the system to explore any topic of interest at your preferred pace and level of detail.

Studies have shown that students derive much benefit from environments which encourage collaborative/cooperative learning. The Web and groupware (such as Lotus Notes) provide opportunities for asynchronous collaboration (participants can share work that may be done at different times and places). Networked writing environments encourage students to write more and to learn from each other. On-line discussion groups can lead to fuller participation in class discussions by students who may not participate in face-to-face classroom environments (Polyson, S., Saltzberg, S., & Goodwin-Jones, R., 1996).

13) Can Expand to Provide Difficult-to-Obtain Reading Materials

There are times when courses are developed before comprehensive literature is available on the topic. The syllabus can include copies of articles you want your students to read, as well as supplemental information not found in course texts. You can include materials that expand on, synthesize, and facilitate critical reflection on issues presented during formal instruction. You might include materials that fill in the gaps not covered by class presentations, or present questions raised by other points of view. When you use the syllabus in this way, be certain that you obtain necessary copyright clearances for reading selections.

14) Can Improve the Effectiveness of Student Note Taking

Good, carefully written notes are a significant resource for active learning. Active thinkers keep notebooks and journals of ideas from readings, lectures, presentations, and their own ruminations about topics. It is important to make every effort to help students improve the quality of this form of writing. As a model, you may want to include outlines that provide an orientation to topics for lectures and presentations, making it clear what you want students to remember, and providing room for their own interpretations and elaborations of the material. You can use notetaking pairs (Johnson, Johnson, & Smith, 1991) intermittently during or at the end of a lecture. (In this case, two students work together to review, add to, or modify their notes. They can use this opportunity to review major concepts and pertinent information, to clarify unresolved issues or concerns.) It is also helpful to include any detailed formulas and diagrams that students will be required to use. You may want to include study techniques that are specific to your course. In this way, the contents of the syllabus will help to organize and focus student notetaking and learning. [See Learning Tools, Part II]

15) Can Include Material that Supports Learning Outside the Classroom

Much learning takes place outside of the classroom. You can transform student study time outside of class by providing strategies in your syllabus that help students to interact more critically with the textbook, supplemental readings, or other work, so that they will be better prepared for class. For example, along with the readings you might give students a short (one page or less) writing assignment that asks them to support, reject, or modify the thesis or claims in the reading. You might include a guide for troubleshooting a story or a drawing. You can also provide self-check assignments that allow students to monitor their progress.

16) Can Serve as a Learning Contract

As an agreement or contract defining mutual obligations between instructor and students, your syllabus also speaks for the college and university. "You should realize that this fact gives you responsibilities but also gives you protection against complaints or challenges to your teaching. For example, the conditions, goals, and requirements you state enable (department chairs and academic administrators) to support your decisions on grades, teaching methods, readings, and topics of inquiry. That is only possible, of course, if you and the administration (and the students) have a record of what you promised and planned, and if your syllabus conforms broadly to program goals and policies" (SU Project Advance, 1995). You will need to be familiar with institutional policies regarding attendance, examinations, drop/adds, course withdrawals, learning disabilities, and academic integrity.

Equipped with an understanding of the myriad ways a learning-centered syllabus can function, you can begin to use it in your course.

Using a Learning-Centered Syllabus

On the first day of class, take the opportunity to introduce and review your syllabus thoroughly, explaining to your students that you have tried to anticipate their learning needs; that this syllabus not only includes the content that you will introduce to support their learning, but also information and tools that they will find useful for active, purposeful, and effective learning in the course. Be sure to allow sufficient time for students to discuss their respective roles as many may be unfamiliar or uncomfortable with active learning and uncertain of your expectations.

> Learners may resist learning procedures that require active engagement with other learners, faculty, or course materials. Constructing and critiquing their own and others' knowledge may contradict their experience and the paradigm that knowledge is something the teacher possesses at the beginning, transmits to students during the course, and that they demonstrate as their own private possession at the end of the course (Wlodkowski & Ginsberg, 1995, p. 286).

You may want to ask your students to review the syllabus outside of class and to write a brief response to the syllabus and the discussion, identifying your role, elaborating their own, and raising any questions that occur to them at this time. If you are using computer technology as a communication tool, you might start the process by asking students to obtain an e-mail account and to send their response to you prior to the next class meeting. If your syllabus is on-line, you may ask them to review this version, noting and responding to the links and other modifications that you have made to the form.

Turn to the syllabus often to encourage students to develop the habit of using it as a common reference throughout the course. Discuss the learning tools that you have included and strategies for their use. If you have included key terms that will be used in discussions or lectures, refer students to the definitions that you have provided and encourage them to locate others or to develop their own definitions as they come to understand the terms more clearly and to connect them to applied contexts. If you have included tools that are intended to help make more useful notes, or to serve as protocols for different types of discussion, refer to them at times when they would be most helpful.

Refer to the syllabus when discussing new assignments. Encourage students to make their own notes elaborating those that you have made for them. Allow time for discussion of assignments. What are the learning objectives for this assignment? How much freedom do students have to learn in their own way? How will the criteria for evaluation be set? Are the criteria clear enough that students will be able to measure their own progress? How do you anticipate the work will proceed, and at what points will you help students to assess their progress?

When approaching tests and examinations or other assessment tools, allow time for questions and suggestions about assessment. Make available examples of concrete learning outcomes that have already been evaluated by the criteria to be used. Including exemplary but realistic examples of other students' accomplishments can clarify your expectations for students and will often inspire students' efforts toward their own work (Wlodkowski & Ginsberg, 1995).

You might want to think of your syllabus as a negotiable contract, a well-considered plan in which you are willing to reinvent some of the structure according to the students and situation you find in your class (Wlodkowski & Ginsberg, 1995). A simple question at mid-term or other appropriate time can elicit much useful information, help you to determine whether revisions are required, and reinforce your expectations for students' responsibility in shaping their education and your interest in their accomplishments.

> Is the way we are conducting class giving you the best chance to learn and demonstrate what you know? (Wlodkowski & Ginsberg, 1995, p. 157). If so, what is most and least useful to you in this regard? If not, what features of the course might we restructure to make this possible, and how?

Your learning-centered syllabus can be a dynamic document that becomes an integral part of your course, that encourages and supports the sort of interactivity, and active, purposeful, effective learning that you want to promote.

Part II
Examples

To help you compose or revise your syllabus with a learning-centered perspective, I have provided examples of sections that you might want to include. However, what you choose to include will depend upon the nature of your students, the type of course you are offering, and the rationale underlying your course. In general, the syllabus should do the following things:

- Describe the course, its goals, and its objectives

- Describe the structure of the course and its significance within the general program of study (particularly any nontraditional aspects of it that may be new to the students)

- Discuss what mutual obligations students and instructors share

- Provide critical logistical and procedural information about what will happen, when, and where

In describing the various sections, I have drawn from materials that were developed by instructors working with the staff of the Center for Instructional Development at Syracuse University and from other sources, as noted. The examples are primarily from undergraduate offerings, including freshman introductory courses and courses offered through distance education. While the examples were not necessarily developed within a framework of learning-centeredness, each contributes something to a learning-centered perspective. I hope they will assist you in designing a learning-centered syllabus that will fit the specific conditions and circumstances in which you and your students work.

CHECKLIST

What you include in your syllabus will be determined by the needs of your students, the type of course you are offering, and the rationale underlying your course. The checklist below can serve as a guide when you prepare your syllabus. Examples of each these items follow.

	Examples	*Page #*
	1. TITLE PAGE	25
	2. TABLE OF CONTENTS	26
	3. INSTRUCTOR INFORMATION	27
	4. LETTER TO THE STUDENT	28
	5. PURPOSE OF THE COURSE	30
	6. COURSE DESCRIPTION	32
	7. COURSE AND UNIT OBJECTIVES	33
	8. RESOURCES	39
	9. READINGS	43
	10. COURSE CALENDAR	45
	11. COURSE REQUIREMENTS	48
	12. EVALUATION	56
	13. GRADING PROCEDURES	65
	14. HOW TO USE THE SYLLABUS	69
	15. HOW TO STUDY FOR THIS COURSE	71
	16. CONTENT INFORMATION	73
	17. LEARNING TOOLS	74

1. Title Page

The title page should include the name and number of the course, the date, and any copyright information needed to protect your work.

Example: Title Page

Course Handbook

Perspectives of Business and Management
SOM 122

The Management Freshman Gateway Course

School of Management
Center for Instructional Development
© Syracuse University, 1995

Adapted from: Perspectives of Business and Management, SOM 122: The Management Freshman Gateway Course. Course Handbook. Theodore O. Wallin, 1994.

2. TABLE OF CONTENTS

If your syllabus is organized as a student reference that will provide the resources of a course manual, it will frequently be read piecemeal. It is, therefore, important to demarcate material and make items easy for students to locate.

The way that you organize your manual will depend upon the content of your course. You may decide to deal with the course as a whole, or it may work better to divide the course into units keeping all the information (i.e., objectives, assignments, evaluations, etc.) separate for each content unit.

EXAMPLE: TABLE OF CONTENTS

Adapted from: Perspectives of Business and Management, SOM 122: The Management Freshman Gateway Course. Course Handbook. Theodore O. Wallin, 1994.

3. INSTRUCTOR INFORMATION

Students should always have a record of the course instructor, where the instructor can be reached, during what hours. This is particularly important when there are several instructors for a course. The record should include anyone else with whom students should be in contact, such as a course TA.

EXAMPLE: INSTRUCTOR INFORMATION

INSTRUCTOR LISTING

COURSE LEADERS

Marjorie Dibble, Professor and Associate Dean
College for Human Development
Office: 112 Slocum Hall   Telephone: 3-4153

RiceMail Address MVDibble @ SUADMIN
Office hours: By appointment

Robert S. Pickett, Professor of Child & Family Studies
College for Human Development
Office: 201A Slocum Hall   Telephone: 3-2757

RiceMail Address: RSPicket @ SUADMIN
Office hours: Tuesday, 10:00–12:00 AM and 3:30–4:30 PM

OTHER HOURS BY APPOINTMENT ONLY

	Section Leader	
	_____Office: _____	
Telephone or Fax: _____RiceMail Address_____		
Office hours:_____		
	Please bring this manual to all lectures and section meetings.	

Adapted from: Human Ecology, CFS 101, College For Human Development. Syracuse University: Center for Instructional Development, Pickett, R. (Ed.), 1993.

4. LETTER TO THE STUDENT

Including a letter to the student in the syllabus enhances the personal nature of the course, can help relieve student discomfort, and can set a dialogic tone for your course.

Some letters are also used to request student involvement in evaluating the course for purposes of improvement. (If you choose to do this, you will want to include also the actual evaluation forms in the course manual.)

EXAMPLE 1: LETTER TO THE STUDENT

I hope you enjoy this course. It is not an easy one. At times, philosophy can seem horribly abstract. At others, it seems too concerned with details. And yet at others, it is hard to see the general point, and to distinguish that point from the twists and turns in the argument. I think, however, every issue taken up here is of fundamental importance—fundamental to a satisfactory and broad view of human life. By fighting through the difficulties, you will be rewarded with insights and perspectives.

I have tried to do two major things in the course: (1) to introduce you to the theories and original writings of some of the greatest thinkers on ethics, and (2) to take up conflicting positions on some current ethical issues. The first goal addresses fundamental principles and fundamental controversies of ethical theory. The second goal is a practical or applied goal—to help you begin to sort out and critically assess the various aspects of current ethical debates over issues that affect our lives.

A side benefit of the theoretical part of the course is that it will strengthen your ability to read difficult but influential texts in the history of ideas. As you wrestle with the vast vocabulary of the great theorists, you will strengthen your own vocabulary and help gain access to other great works that have shaped the modern world.

Good luck to you.

Sincerely,

Adapted from: Student Guide for Ethics: Theories and Controversies. A Syracuse University independent study course. Syracuse University: Center for Instructional Development, Thau, S., 1992.

EXAMPLE 2: LETTER TO THE STUDENT

Welcome to CFS 101, a very special course in the College for Human Development. It is the first course that you will take within the college and the only one in which all freshmen, regardless of program, will be together. In this course, you will attend two lectures or large group presentations each week. Once a week you will attend section meetings, dedicated to small group discussion and work sessions with the faculty and other students. The large group presentations will focus on the transition from adolescence to adulthood and the kinds of issues that you and your peers are likely to deal with during this phase of your life and during the years immediately following graduation. Previous freshmen classes have been surveyed, and faculty have been consulted to determine what would be important to include in these presentations. Their opinions and advice, as well as the specific strengths of this college, have been taken into account in selecting the discussion topics.

Although the large presentation sessions and small section meetings will often be dealing with the same subject matter, you must regard the large group meetings as essentially separate from what goes on in the small sections. Your section leader may comment on the readings related to the large presentations, but do not expect that he or she will discuss the lectures. Much of the time spent in the section meetings will be devoted to working on the skills necessary for achieving success in college. Your section leader will provide a separate syllabus for the activities and assignments to be carried out in your section and will submit an independent grade that will be averaged with the grade for the large group portion of the course.

Instead of a textbook, you are expected to purchase a packet that includes this manual, a book of readings, and a computer instruction manual. The first part of this course manual (the white pages) has been designed to provide information about your responsibilities and assignments in the large group sessions. The remainder of the manual (the blue pages) provides you with basic material you need for small section activities. Read both parts carefully and follow the instructions diligently.

The responsibility for meeting course requirements is one you must assume. If you attend to this responsibility with care, we believe you will be successful in the course and will start your college career in a very positive fashion.

Best wishes!

Adapted from: Human Ecology, CFS 101, College For Human Development. Syracuse University: Center for Instructional Development, Pickett, R. (Ed.), 1993.

5. PURPOSE OF THE COURSE

The section of the syllabus that addresses the purpose of the course should focus on why the course exists, how it fits into the larger curriculum, and for whom it was designed. If from the start students know what you are trying to accomplish, they can be invited to discuss and clearly understand course goals so that you can pursue them together.

EXAMPLE 1: PURPOSE OF THE COURSE

Welcome to SOM 122! This Gateway course enrolls all entering students in the School of Management and is designed to provide an introduction to the School of Management, the study of management, and management careers. You will be involved in various activities in this class to build your familiarity in these areas. We hope you will find it a challenging and enriching experience.

Adapted from: Perspectives of Business and Management, SOM 122: The Management Freshman Gateway Course. Course Handbook. Theodore O. Wallin, 1994.

EXAMPLE 2: PURPOSE OF THE COURSE

The purpose of this course is to introduce the student to the theory, purposes, and methods of Financial Accounting on an introductory level. Here are some of the benefits you will get from the successful completion of this course.

- This course, offered as the introductory accounting course at colleges and universities, will give you a foundation for further work in accounting. The course will give you a feel for what accounting is about and its level of difficulty. Of course, the type of employment one can expect is dependent on the amount of schooling one obtains. A four-year degree is required for many accounting jobs.

- You will gain a minimum level knowledge of accounting that can be used in financial statement analysis. It should be kept in mind, however, that a little knowledge can be dangerous. The knowledge required to be successful at investing in stocks and bonds goes far beyond that which is included in this course and also includes areas of knowledge outside accounting. You will be able to read the financial press and financial statements with more understanding and make more knowledgeable financial decisions as a result of taking this course.

- This course will give you a basic understanding of a form of business communication. Upon successful completion of this course, you will be able to look at a set of financial statements, understand their components, and have a basic understanding of how the financial statement numbers were produced.

- This course will help satisfy the curiosity of anyone who wonders about the meaning behind all the numbers and concepts that drive businesses all over the world.

Adapted from: Financial Accounting Systems. Student Manual. Badr Ismail and Donald Slocum, 1993.

6. COURSE DESCRIPTION

This section of the syllabus provides students with an overview of the course and may provide an explanation of how the course will be conducted (i.e., lectures, small group discussion, project teams, field experiences, simulations, etc.).

EXAMPLE 1: COURSE DESCRIPTION

Understanding history provides a basis for coming to terms with the complexity and significance of a region where two World Wars began. American troops may be called upon to act in the conflict in former Yugoslavia, and the future security of Europe is inextricably tied to developments in this region.

This course will address Eastern Europe's tempestuous history from the end of the first World War until the present. The introduction will provide a brief overview of the empires that once dominated Eastern Europe. Units 1–8 will explore the formation of fledgling nation-states from the ruins of empires to the vortex of the Second World War. Unit 9 of the course deals with Eastern Europe in the conflagration of World War II. The transformation from fascism to communism, the collapse of communism, and the current transitions are examined in Units 10–19 of the course.

Adapted from: Eastern European History—From Independence to Independence: 1918 to the Present. Walter Ullmann and Jonathan P.G. Bach, 1993.

EXAMPLE 2: COURSE DESCRIPTION

The course begins with an overview of the financial statements and the introduction of the accounting cycle. The underlying theory of recording accounting transactions is introduced and the student is taught how the financial statements are built up through the accounting process. The course also looks at individual sections of the financial statements on a more detailed level. Most of the text concentrates on elements of the balance sheet, though the income statement and statements of cash flow are covered as well. You will quickly realize that accounting is a fairly complex process with considerable flexibility in its application.

Adapted from: Financial Accounting Systems. Student Manual. Badr Ismail and Donald Slocum, 1993.

EXAMPLE 3: COURSE DESCRIPTION

This is a research seminar. It's a course about ideas and how to investigate them. We will explore a specific, deeply philosophical question in the world of ideas comparing two very different visions with respect to the question: "What factors shape our behavior?"—and we will research an historical question: "What factors shaped the labor force behavior of women from the pre to the post World War II period?" assessing the relative strengths and weaknesses of the two visions we will explore.

Our method (there is method in our madness) will be to study the ideas and to research the history in parallel. There will be readings from the economics and the sociology literature on the determinates of human behavior. We will hold class discussions to insure that everyone understands the readings and to explore the ideas represented in these readings. At the same time everyone will be engaged in the historical research (more on this process below). Our first classes will be devoted to getting everyone started on the historical research, and subsequently one class each week will be devoted to sharing information and tips that will help everyone make progress on the research project.

Adapted from: Understanding Rosie the Riveter: Research Seminar on Values and Choices, ECN 204. Jerry Evensky, Spring 1997.

7. COURSE AND UNIT OBJECTIVES

An important function of your syllabus is to indicate to students what it is that they will be accountable for in your course—what they will have to do, and under what conditions. Students should be able to find out where your course leads intellectually and practically, what they will know by the end of the course, and how they will be expected to demonstrate what they have learned. Is one of the purposes of the course to improve their problem solving abilities? improve their communication skills? allow them to translate knowledge from one context to another? Why are the goals important, and how will different parts of the course help students accomplish those goals?

Objectives make goals more specific, providing a basic plan for what is to be accomplished and how that should be evaluated in students. Objectives can be written at a course or unit level. They may be of two different types:

- Concrete statements of what students will be able to do as the result of learning.

- Open ended, flexible descriptions of a situation or problem out of which various kinds of learning might arise (Davis, 1993b). Objectives then would be expectations that delimit the direction of the students but do not predefine an endpoint for their learning or try to guarantee a particular interpretation or outcome. You would let more specific objectives emerge as they are appropriate to the individual student in resolving the task.

EXAMPLE 1: COURSE OBJECTIVES

Goals for the Capstone Course

In spring of 1989, the capstone course development team began meeting to define course objectives and instructional approaches for a capstone course. We met with department heads and others who were both interested and expert in the subject of crop management and interdisciplinary education. We were assured of departmental support and provided with good guidance about topics of importance to a senior-level, "put it all together" course.

We identified five course objectives for students:

1. Improved competence and confidence in problem identification and in using technically sound, analytical approaches to problem solving

2. Improved ability to exercise judgment and assess options in crop management

3. Improved ability to use team approaches to problem solving and decision-making

4. Improved ability to describe and defend problem analyses and management decisions both orally and in writing

5. Greater understanding of principal management considerations involved in a wide array of agronomic and horticultural cropping systems

As the course outcomes took shape, it became evident that most related to objectives other than the attainment of new knowledge. It was clear from the beginning that this course would emphasize problem analysis, application of technical knowledge, and the student's capacity

to make sound decisions. We determined that students in this capstone course should have a decidedly interdisciplinary experience and engage in management problems encompassing a wide array of agronomic and horticultural cropping systems. With the support of college and departmental administrators, it was agreed that the multi-departmental faculty responsible for the course would jointly instruct it. Thus the course was to feature a truly integrated, interdisciplinary approach.

Adapted from Simmons, S.R. (1995). Using Decision Cases in a Capstone Course. In Lunde, J.P. (Ed.). Reshaping Curricula: Revitalization Programs at Three Land Grant Universities. *Bolton, MA: Anker Publishing Company.*

EXAMPLE 2: COURSE OBJECTIVES

Goals

The areas of visual communication contain several aspects, not the least of which are the processes and technologies that exist for artists to conceive and execute printed communications. In industry, it is not enough to have a great idea: It is mandatory to develop the skills required to generate ideas into finished products.

The objective of this course is to continue to learn how to use the computer as a tool for creating comprehensive layouts and/or mechanicals for pre-press production. It will be highly technical, as opposed to highly creative, and using the software well is critical to the success of the product. In addition, we will look at some traditional (analog) skills and processes, and combine appropriate uses of these skills into the final presentation for each project.

Short-term, you will develop work habits and skills required by the other courses in your area of study.

Mid-term, you will have a marketable portfolio for a summer job or internship.

Long-term, you will develop the skills and work habits required by professionals within the industry. These skills will qualify you for entry-level, or better, job opportunities.

Your ultimate goal is computer literacy, specifically as it relates to the design and communications industry. That means not only will you continue to learn how a Mac works, but also explore in greater depth the programs or applications which will help you create text, images, and page layouts. These skills will serve you through the balance of your academic career in producing work for other VisCom classes, and proficiency with communications and design software will put you at an advantage when seeking your first job—most agencies and design firms are actively seeking graduates with computer skills.

Objectives

Develop manual skills in the use of drafting tools and materials and appropriate applications.

Develop professional work ethics, including precision, neatness, ability to follow instructions and meet deadlines, and appropriate use of problem solving skills.

Develop capabilities in design using text and image, including composition, proportion, color, surface, information hierarchies, and formats.

Develop skills and sensitivity in typographic design, page design, image development, and rendering text and image using both digital and analog tools.

Understand traditional pre-press and printing technologies and develop the skills required for basic pre-press production.

Adapted from: Design Skills and Processes, CMD 282. Toni Toland, 1996.

EXAMPLE 3: COURSE OBJECTIVES

SOM 122 focuses on the prevailing management trend towards skills required for effective conduct in the business world. You will see that attention is given to teamwork, oral presentations, writing, computer skills, and social skills that are connected with being part of a large institution. SOM 122 has the following learning objectives.

When you have completed this course, you should be able to:

1. Identify the skills that are necessary for success in business.

2. Understand how the skills necessary for success in business are applied in the "real world."

3. Create a plan for developing business skills while at Syracuse University.

4. Understand fundamental issues that arise when working in small teams.

5. Plan and carry out a project with a team, developing teamwork skills.

6. Develop skills of analyzing an audience and tailoring written and oral reports to their interests and needs.

7. Use the SU on-line catalog to access library collections, services, and resources.

8. Research career information and become acquainted with relevant books, academic journals, and trade journals.

9. Cite sources in a written report, construct a bibliography, and discuss and evaluate the views of other authors.

10. Understand the concept of "computer system" as a means to an end in learning and in business.

11. Locate the essential computer facilities available to students on campus.

12. Use the two basic software application packages in the SU PC clusters: word processing and Pine (electronic mail).

13. Accomplish a smooth transition to college.

14. Build a strong identity with the School of Management and a solid direction for your future studies and career plans.

Adapted from: Perspectives of Business and Management, SOM 122: The Management Freshman Gateway Course. Course Handbook. Theodore O. Wallin, 1994.

EXAMPLE 4: UNIT OBJECTIVES

Goals

1. To explore and reflect on a large philosophical question: How are the values that shape our choices in life determined?

2. To learn how to effectively and efficiently research a question and present a coherent and persuasive representation of your thoughts in an answer.

3. To explore the choices made by women who moved into and then out of the traditionally male sector of the labor market during World War II: to understand Rosie the Riveter.

Objectives

To thoughtfully address the following questions: Do we learn to value/choose from our social context (are values social?), do we determine what we value/choose by how things or people serve our self interest (are values economic?), or is there another way of thinking of values and choices?

To understand two classic stories about values and choices: A classic economic story represented by the work of Gary Becker (Nobel Prize winner in economics), and a classic social story represented by Berger and Luckmann's book *The Social Construction of Reality.*

To develop your ability to research a topic and present your findings; e.g., find useful sources, take effective and useful notes, develop a logical presentation and outline it, write a good paper presenting your ideas.

To write a high quality research paper on the choices made by women who moved into and then out of the traditionally male sector of the labor market during World War II.

Adapted from: Understanding Rosie the Riveter: Research Seminar on Values and Choices, ECN 204. Jerry Evensky, Spring 1997.

EXAMPLE 5: UNIT OBJECTIVES

Writing Studio I Module 2: Joining the Discussion
Here are the goals for this module:

- To build on the "writing to learn" exercises we began in Module 1.

- To use summarizing, paraphrasing, and excerpting effectively to place your own opinion in the context of others.

- To develop complex opinions that take into account the subtleties and differing assumptions of a number of other positions.

- To express your own opinion in a way that explicitly responds to the opinions of others.

- To work on issues of technical control discovered in Module 1.

For each of the first three sections in this module, you will read a selection from Readings for Writing Studio I and respond to it in a number of ways, each designed to enhance your understanding of the reading and to develop your own position. In the final two sections you will write a formal argumentative paper.

Adapted from: Writing Studio I. Course Guide. Nance Hahn, 1994.

EXAMPLE 6: UNIT OBJECTIVES

Writing Studio Module 4: Re-vision, Reflection, and Celebration
Through the final cycle of revision, the construction of the portfolio, reflection on what you've done, and assessment of both yourself and the course, we expect you will:

- Develop an understanding of revision that is complex and notably different from your earlier concept of revision. By the end of this module, distinctions among revising, editing, and proofreading will stand out clearly in your mind.

- Observe your own literacy development and hypothesize and theorize about it, with particular attention to your growth in the kinds of writing, reading, and thinking you need to excel in college study.

- Begin to assess and take personal responsibility for your own literacy learning.

- Improve the course by sharing your impressions and suggestions.

Adapted from: Writing Studio I. Course Guide. Nance Hahn, 1994.

8. RESOURCES

The purpose of the resource section is to guide students to course resources and encourage their use. Course resources can include published materials, individuals such as librarians or other faculty, media centers, etc. This section should list all materials that will be needed for the course as well as their location (i.e., the college bookstore, the reserve room at the library, the computer lab, etc.). If you are using a lab or resource room, you will need to tell the students where it is located, when it is open, and how they are to use it. You might also explain why books and other resources have been chosen and what their relative importance is to the course or discipline.

EXAMPLE 1: RESOURCES

You will benefit in this course by access to *written materials* and to *people*. The written materials (available in the Syracuse University Bookstore) are as follows:

Course Handbook—This handbook provides you with essential information about the course, electronic mail instruction, and some exercises and requirements.

Management: A Total Quality Perspective Bounds, Dobbins, & Fowler—This book is the primary text for the course. Reading assignments are listed on the Schedule of Class Meetings in this handbook (pp. 10–11).

Majoring in the Rest of Your Life by Carter

Introduction to Microsoft Word for Windows 6.0

Campbell Interest Survey

Equally important are the people that you will be meeting and working with. The following people are available to you throughout the course; we encourage you to consult them at any point in the semester:

- **Section leader**—A member of the School of Management faculty or staff will direct your section meetings and work with you on your team project and other section activities. *He or she will also serve as your academic advisor for the first two years of your work here.*

- **TA**—Each section will have a teaching assistant, a sophomore student in the School of Management, who will act as a resource person for you and your section leader.

- **Professor Wallin**—Professor Wallin is coordinator of SOM 122 and will chair the class meetings, introduce the speakers, and direct class activities. He also serves as a section leader. As Director of the Freshman Experience in the School of Management, he is an overall resource person to you in your freshman and sophomore years. Bring him any questions that have not been resolved by your section leader, TA, or GA. Professor Wallin can be found in Room 212, School of Management.

- **Peer advisor**—You will have an upper-class peer advisor from the School of Management. He or she can be a valuable resource to help you become acclimated to the School of Management and to Syracuse University.

- **Alumni-mentor**—The alumni-mentor is a professional person in the Syracuse community who has volunteered to work with a small group in your class to acquaint you with the Syracuse community.

- **Undergraduate Office**—In Room 210 you will find the Undergraduate Office for the School of Management. The staff members in this office can answer questions about registration, the maintenance of your academic records, appeals, adding or dropping classes, and other basic academic concerns. They will maintain your file and become the final arbiters on decisions that need to be made about your academic program. The office is open during regular academic hours.

- **Syracuse University Business Club (SubC)**—a freshman-oriented student organization that seeks to conduct outside of class activities to enrich the management experience of our freshmen.

These people provide a wide support system for you. Feel free to ask for their office or residence location, their available hours, and their help in resolving matters of concern. You can also contact them through e-mail.

Learning to use resources creatively is one of the essentials of effective management.

Adapted from: Perspectives of Business and Management, SOM 122: The Management Freshman Gateway Course. Course Handbook. Theodore O. Wallin, 1994.

EXAMPLE 2: RESOURCES

Materials & Supplies

Purchase, if you have not already done so, a 44MB SyQuest (or comparable) disk. Available at SUB, Barnes & Noble, and other good bookstores are some recommended books, like the *Mac Bible*. Please see the attached bibliography for some titles. Since there is no textbook for this course, and no instruction manuals for the software we use, it would be smart to buy at least one third party book for each program we cover. I have indicated my personal favorites with an *.

In addition, there will be times when you will need to purchase some "analog" materials (things you use at a drawing table). I will give you lists and demonstrate the use of these materials at that time.

Lab Fees

The lab fee you paid for this course covers the maintenance and repair or replacement of equipment in the cluster, purchase of software, revisions and updates, providing open hours for computer use outside of class, and b&w printing. It also subsidizes the cost of photostats and shrinkwrapping, which you may use in the presentation of your projects.

The Shaffer Cluster

While we hope the cluster runs smoothly most of the time, there will be times when problems occur. Please notify any supervising person immediately and BE PATIENT. It is also advisable to save everything you do frequently, and to make back-up discs of all your work. The *Mac Bible* or another generic Mac book would be a tremendous value as a resource for correcting problems on your own . . . I highly recommend owning one. (see Bibliography)

This cluster is not a public cluster; your non-VisCom friends and/or roommates are not allowed to use it. The cluster serves not only this class, but 10 others, and during open hours (which are posted) it provides resources to all other VisCom majors and Computer Graphics majors as well. Please abide by the posted rules and the cluster monitors' requests. If there are any problems which result from your negligence or interference, you will earn an "F" for the semester.

VPA has its own server with multiple copies of all the software we will be studying this semester (and then some!). This means that you can log on to this server from any other Mac Cluster on campus to get work done. So far, the only drawback to this is the inconvenience in accessing all the fonts we use here in the cluster. To log on to the VPA Server, choose it from the chooser (Appleshare . . . Crouse Zone . . . MacApps).

Use _____ as your user name and _____ as your password. Do not share this information with anyone else: if they log on before you, you will not be able to get access to the software you need!

It is against the law to copy software. It is also against cluster policy to load software onto any computer, or to attach any external hardware to them. Anyone found doing so will flunk this course, and have all cluster privileges rescinded for the balance of his/her academic career (that means until you graduate). Don't do it.

Adapted from: Design Skills and Processes, CMD 282. Toni Toland, 1996.

EXAMPLE 3: RESOURCES

Reading Resources

By now, you should have purchased the packet that includes a copy of the *CFS 101 Human Ecology Readings* booklet from the Syracuse University Bookstore. These readings are meant to accompany and support the various presentations of the course. They are organized according to the sequence of lectures found later in this manual. The readings should be read prior to each presentation session.

Other outside readings will be assigned, from time to time, from the *reading reserve section* on the second floor of Bird Library. When such readings are assigned, please consult the set of loose-leaf notebooks on the tables in the reading reserve section. Supplementary lists of readings for courses (arranged alphabetically by the last name of Course Leaders) are included in these notebooks, and you can request the specific reading from the librarian at the reserve desk.

Adapted from: Human Ecology, CFS 101, College For Human Development. Syracuse University: Center for Instructional Development, Pickett, R. (Ed.), 1993.

9. Readings

Your syllabus may include readings for the course. Students will appreciate having all the materials at hand. The selected readings can be included as part of the syllabus or can be produced as a separate volume. The examples provide a guide to the readings. When you use the syllabus in this way, be *certain* that you obtain necessary copyright clearances.

EXAMPLE 1: GUIDE TO THE READINGS

I want to take a moment to clarify how I hope you will approach the readings. The first rule is: Don't take the readings as gospel. Just because something is printed does not make it Absolute Truth. Be critical of what you are reading, drawing upon your own experiences and other knowledge. I have chosen many readings precisely because they are provocative. If you find yourself strongly disagreeing with a particular reading, that's fine; indeed, I encourage strong disagreement. *However,* if you disagree, you must clarify in your mind the reasons and evidence upon which you are basing your disagreement.

At the same time, keep an open mind. Listen to what the readings have to say. Think about what other experiences you have had and reading you have done that might corroborate the course readings. Give yourself time to *reflect* on the information, insights, and perspectives offered in the readings. These are not readings to be run through rapidly. Take your time with them; allow yourself to enter into a kind of conversation with them.

Adapted from: Eastern European History—From Independence to Independence: 1918 to the Present. Walter Ullmann and Jonathan P.G. Bach, 1993.

EXAMPLE 2: READINGS

Readings for the Writing Studio

We put a good deal of effort into selecting the readings, and we believe the pieces we have here will help us to accomplish the work of WRT 115 while at the same time providing intellectual stimulation and entertainment. Later in the course we'll ask you how you feel about our choices.

Each of the course readings can work for you in at least two ways. They provide content—new knowledge, or at least a new perspective on a topic with which you may already be familiar. Further, the readings serve as examples of the kinds of writing you yourself will be doing. For instance, in the first section of the course, where we ask you to write about your own reading and writing experiences, we provide essays in which the authors are going about the very same business. Later, in the third module, we ask you to observe some facets of life around you and to write about and interpret what you see. Then we supply chapters from books which work on that very project. Beyond that, all of the readings are examples of different kinds of good writing, writing we hope you will savor, study, and choose at times to emulate. So look through the readings, see which writers you've heard of and which will constitute unexplored territory, sample sentences here and there, and whet your appetite. Then turn your attention back to this Course Guide and read the module descriptions.

Adapted from: Writing Studio I. Course Guide. Nance Hahn, 1994.

10. Course Calendar

A course calendar indicating topics or activities planned for each class meeting, assignment due dates, and special occasions or events is very helpful to students. Calendars can be arranged on various levels including class, section, etc. Students should be cautioned about the tentative nature of such calendars and should clearly understand how revised timetables or plans will be communicated.

Example 1: Course Calendar

Schedule and Assignments

Week	Date	Topic	Assignment*
1	8/30	Introduction—Nature of Management	Carter Ch. 1
2	9/6	Functions and Skills of Management Total Quality Management	Massie & Douglas Ch. 1, 2
3	9/13	Dilemmas in Management: Ethics	M&D, Ch. 3
4	9/20	Teamwork Concepts—Panel of Former Students	M&D, Ch. 13, 14
5	9/27	The Manager as Problem Solver	M&D, Ch. 5, 6
6	10/4	Managing Technology & Innovation	M&D Ch. 17,18
7	10/11	The Manager as Change Agent Research Plan due	M&D Ch. 16
8	10/18	Conflict Resolution & Management	M&D Ch. 15
9	10/2	Coping With Stress and Time Management	Carter Ch. 4
10	11/1	Registration and Developing a Specific Direction For Your Career	Carter Ch. 2, 3
11	11/8	Teamwork: Practitioner View	M&D Ch. 7
12	11/15	Effective Communications	M&D Ch. 10
13	11/22	The Global Manager	M&D Ch. 3
14	11/29	Leadership Styles for the Twenty-First Century	M&D Ch. 9
15	12/6	**Section Meeting (Tuesday)**	Presentations
16	12/8	Grand Finale: Reviewing the Semester & Looking Ahead (Thursday)	M&D Ch. 19 Carter Ch. 7, 13 Final Exam Due

*Additional assignments may be given.

Other Key Dates—You will be expected to attend the following events:
9/ 22—10:30–3:30 SU's Career Fair in Schine's Goldstein Auditorium.
10/29—School of Management Open House 10:00–2:00
11/4—School of Management 75th Anniversary Forum
    in the SOM Auditorium—9:00–11:45 & 2:00–4:30

Adapted from: Perspectives of Business and Management, SOM 122: The Management Freshman Gateway Course. Course Handbook. Theodore O. Wallin, 1994.

EXAMPLE 2: COURSE CALENDAR

Monday, January 23/Cluster

In class: lecture and hands-on practice with Quark XPress (4 page layout)

- *4 page layout:* I will provide you with text and images, and a hand rendered layout for a brochure. You job will be to translate it into a Quark XPress document that accurately resembles the hand drawn comp.

  This is due at the end of class today, as a file saved to CMD 282 folder on the VisCom server.

Homework:

- *Generate hardcopy for 4 page layout:* Mount, flap, and mark up for printer. Due mounted and flapped by 2:00, marked up for printer by 5:00 next week.

- *Develop rough layouts (3) for typographic poster/ad:* Choose one issue about which you are passionate. Develop a position on your issue and create three different single page layouts which will convince those who see it to change their minds, if they don't already agree with you. This layout is limited to text only, so choose your font(s) wisely and create a solid, exciting layout with the text you write. Remember that your headline must immediately arrest people who walk by, or turn to this page in a publication and convince them to read further. Finished size is tabloid (11" x 17") either horizontal or vertical.

Monday, January 30/classroom

In class: demo on marking up artwork for printer critique of typographic poster roughs

- *4 page layout:* Due as hard copy, mounted and flapped and marked up for the printer by 5:00

- *Typographic poster/ad:* 3 rough layouts due today at 2:00 for in-class crit. A revised layout will be due next week.

Homework:

- *Revise typographic poster/ad:* Based on in-class critiques, improve on your layout and create new rough. Mount this rough on illustration board and flap.

Monday, February 6/cluster

In class: review of type options in Adobe Illustrator and hands-on practice (typographic poster/ad)

- *Typographic poster/ad:* Using your final rough as a guide, begin to create a finished poster/ad using Adobe Illustrator, and Quark XPress. Due next week...

Homework:

- *Choose vacation spot and begin research for text and images:* Research a vacation spot: write text which includes information on its climate, special events (festivals, etc.), special sights and activities (i.e. architecture, museums, shopping, leisure activities), and information on how to obtain more information; assemble and/or create appropriate images. Resources for your research should include magazines, library books and articles, travel agencies. You may use existing images from these resources with appropriate credit lines. (HINT: It would be smart to choose a place you have already been to, or one to which you would like to go!) You will design a 6 page brochure no larger than 14" x 17" unfolded (tabloid size) using the text and images you develop.

- *Typographic poster/ad:* Finish layout in Quark XPress, output in color or black & white (as appropriate), mount on foam core, and have shrink wrapped. File should be saved in CMD 282 folder on server no later than midnight Thursday, February 9th.

- *Self portrait:* Locate or have a photograph of yourself taken and developed. Yearbook or composite photos are most appropriate.

Adapted from: Design Skills and Processes, CMD 282. Toni Toland, 1996.

11. COURSE REQUIREMENTS

Students should be informed about the expectations for each course assignment and project.

EXAMPLE 1: COURSE REQUIREMENTS

Writing the Papers

The course requires you to write fourteen papers. There will be no formal exams. Your papers should each be about three to four typed pages or four to six handwritten pages. Each paper is assigned after you have completed the readings and exercises for a pair of lessons, and each paper is designed to get you to think about those two lessons; i.e., to think in comparative terms about, on the one hand, American culture, and, on the other, the values and practices of a certain Nonwestern society.

The papers are an opportunity for you to thoughtfully engage the material for this course. Do your best to make the papers coherent and well-argued. It is never enough to simply say that you think something is wrong or right. You must be able to develop an argument about it. How valuable is an opinion if you cannot rationally persuade others?

The papers *must* demonstrate that you have carried out the readings, generally by referring to key positions or arguments expressed by the assigned authors. Of course, you should also draw upon your own experience and, if applicable, other readings. But remember, you must show us in your papers that you've done the reading.

Adapted from: Global Encounters: Comparing Western and Nonwestern Cultures. John Burdick, Yamuna Sangarasivam, and Tanya Cohen, 1994.

EXAMPLE 2: COURSE REQUIREMENTS

Like all courses, this class has specific requirements. You are required to attend lectures on Tuesday afternoons and to participate in small section meetings on Thursday afternoons. Each section will be directed by a faculty or staff member. In these section meetings you will be assigned to a team that will undertake a semester-long project involving library research, interviews, and oral and written reports. In addition to the group project, you will be asked to do readings, complete in- and out-of-class graded assignments, take quizzes, take a final examination, and take part in computer exercises. You will find details of assignments and class activities in this handbook. Information on your examinations will be provided in class.

Adapted from: Perspectives of Business and Management, SOM 122: The Management Freshman Gateway Course. Course Handbook. Theodore O. Wallin, 1994.

EXAMPLE 3: THE RESEARCH PROCESS

Background

Research is not a cookie cutter process. It requires a subtle and creative application of mind, for even as you are developing your project—finding evidence, constructing a story—you must constantly be on the look-out for holes in your logic that make you move back to the search for more sources of evidence, or turns in your understanding that make you rethink and recast your unfolding story—which in turn might lead you down new search paths for evidence, or surprises that allow your mind to make creative leaps to a new richness in the story you are developing. Notice the use of the word story? Research is not about Truth with a capital "T." It's about your understanding of truth, about your vision of how the world works. The sturdiness of your story will be tested by the challenges of those with alternative stories to tell. The way to build a sturdy story is to find as much solid evidence as you can and to weave that evidence into a coherent and compelling story.

Because research is a process of finding, weaving, assessing, tearing, finding, reweaving... it is not a process that can be isolated into a two hour block here, or a twenty minute block there. Good research is an ongoing process that occupies a continuous space in your mind. Sometimes you will be in the library actively searching for sources, for evidence to build or remake your story. Sometimes you'll be at a word processor developing the vision that seemed so seamless and ingenious in your mind's eye into a story that will have to satisfy the real eye of a skeptic reading your printed page—no mean feat. But more often than not, it will occupy a place in the remote recesses of your mind—not on your mind, but not out of your mind—at the ready for some comment, some scene, some moment of current experience that sparks a thought on the project, and immediately it will be called forward—front and center—to be explored and developed in light of this small or large explosion of thought.

Doing research by cookie cutter in blocks of grudgingly committed time is a real drudge and often a real pain. Doing research as one intellectually engaged and committed to telling a good, creative, well-documented story is a fascinating adventure (travel to distant places, times, and minds), a lot of fun (have you ever dreamed of being a detective or a private eye or a investigative reporter or . . .), and very satisfying (be the first on your subject to see the world in a new and compelling way).

If you're going to be in this class, you will be required to do a research project. If you take it on as a cookie cutter process in blocks of grudgingly committed time, it will be a real drudge and often a real pain, and probably you will not be very successful. In that case this might not be the best class for you. If you commit yourself to being intellectually engaged and to telling a good, creative, well-documented story, I think you'll find the trip through history fascinating and the trip through your mind a very rewarding experience. If you do the job on this latter basis, there is no way you can lose.

Adapted from: Understanding Rosie the Riveter: Research Seminar on Values and Choices, ECN 204. Jerry Evensky, Spring 1997.

EXAMPLE 4: PROJECTS

You will be required to complete up to eight projects this semester. In addition to these, there may or may not be tests. These will factor into your grade as projects—that is, they will carry the same weight as a writing, design, or illustration assignment. Each project you do will be handed in twice: once as appropriately presented hard copy (printed on the laserwriter, or on the Fiery . . .) and the second as a file saved to the appropriate folder on the VisCom/AMS server. IMPORTANT: If you do not attach your name to the file when saving to the server, I will not grade it, and it will be counted as late.

2   All type poster/ad
program: Quark Xpress, Adobe Illustrator
objective: use of XPress and Illustrator to create text and design a page

presentation
format: color hard copy, mounted on foam core and shrink-wrapped; file saved to CMD 282 folder on VisCom server

description: Choose an issue about which you are passionate. Develop a position on your issue and create a single page which will convince those who see it to change their minds, if they don't already agree with you.

This page is limited to text only, so choose your font(s) wisely and create a solid, exciting layout with the text you write. Remember that your headline must immediately arrest people who walk by, or turn to this page in a newspaper, and convince them to read further. Finished size is tabloid (11" x 17") either horizontal or vertical.

3 Self portrait

program: Adobe Photoshop & Illustrator
objective: use of Photoshop capabilities including filters, channels, exporting paths, importing art from Adobe Illustrator
presentation
format: color output, mounted on foam core and shrinkwrapped
description: This will be more fun than serious: an opportunity for you to use Photoshop and Illustrator to manipulate a picture of yourself, adding a background and generally discovering some of the features of Photoshop and Illustrator. Finished image size will be 6" x 9" (on 8.5" x 11" paper), mounted on foam core and shrinkwrapped.

4 Six-page vacation brochure

program: XPress, Photoshop, Illustrator
objective: more XPress, with the opportunity to explore your own page design and folding options; research, and text & image development; creating and formatting files in Photoshop and Illustrator for use in XPress
presentation
format: color output, mounted in 3d dummy format; folder with document file and all attendant image files saved to CMD 282 folder on VisCom server
description: Research a vacation spot: write text which includes information on its climate, special events (festivals, etc.), special sights and activities (i.e. architecture, museums, shopping,

leisure activities), and information on how to obtain more information (list of hotels, restaurants, etc.); assemble and/or create appropriate images. Resources for your research should include magazines, library books and articles, travel agencies. You may use existing images from these resources with appropriate credit lines. (HINT: It would be smart to choose a place you have already been to, or one to which you would like to go.)

Design a six-page brochure no larger than 14" x 17" unfolded (tabloid size) using the text and images you develop.

6, 7, & ...

The rest of the projects of this semester will be determined based on degree of skill and development. They may be remedial, they may take the form of tests, or they may be additional parts to previous projects.

Adapted from: Design Skills and Processes, CMD 282. Toni Toland, 1996.

EXAMPLE 5: GROUP WORK

Forming Groups
Members
I will assign groups based on a survey regarding self-assessment of individual strengths and weaknesses. You may indicate on the survey if there are people you would like to work with, and I will take that into consideration, but in the last analysis I will make assignments based on the interests of the class as a whole. In this survey I will ask if you would like to be considered for the position of group coordinator. If you choose not to do so, I would appreciate it if you would identify any classmate(s) whom you believe would be an effective group coordinator.

Group Coordinator
Each group will have a Group Coordinator. The job of the coordinator is to insure the effective functioning of the group by organizing and leading meetings, facilitating discussion, guiding the synthesis of ideas, and producing the presentation. The Group Coordinator is also responsible for keeping me informed of progress and any problems in the group. The Group Coordinator's "Period Piece" will be different from those of the group members—it should be an historical overview of the time, and of the field at the time in question. The quality of leadership

by the coordinator will be considered in the final grade of each person who serves in that role: a good job will help; irresponsibility will hurt.

Group Presentation—A Description
Objective
The objective of this group activity is to create a discourse about ideas within the group and to provide interesting insights into the topic for the rest of the class.

Group assignment
Each group will be responsible for preparing and presenting to the class (during one class session), one of the periods we will study. In order to accomplish this each group member must:

1. Identify common times that all group members can set aside for potential group meetings. Anyone who cannot accommodate such a time may have to do the enhanced paper option (see below).

2. Maintain ongoing communication with other group members about group activities.

3. Immediately read the materials assigned for the group's presentation topic.

4. Identify one economist (broadly defined as anyone writing about econ) from the period covered by the group topic as the individual about whom s/he will write his/her "Period Piece" paper (see below).

5. Read and provide a one or two page written critique of the "Period Piece" papers by other members of the group.

6. Identify, in concert with the other members of your group, a theme/issue/talking point/. . . to be developed into a group presentation.

7. Share responsibility for the production and implementation of a presentation on the period assigned to the group. The first goal is to be effective in offering an interesting and educational experience; another is to be creative and to encourage discussion.

8. Participate in the group presentation.

9. Complete the project assessment.

Assessment
After the group presentation each individual will submit:

1. A one page descriptive self-assessment (what individual activities one undertook to contribute to the group and how one worked to make the group function well as a group) and a summary grade (from 0 to 20, with 18–20 being the A range, 16–17 the B range, 14–15 the C range, 12–13 the D range, and so on).

2. A one page commentary on the contribution of others in the group to the group's success (e.g., quality of commentaries, attendance at group meetings, effort, effectiveness, leadership, creativity), including numeric assessment based on the scale above.

   Assessments of individual's "Group Contribution" will be based on these internal assessments and my judgment of the group performance.

In Case of Non-cooperative or Destructive Behavior

If, in my judgment, any member of a group fails to cooperate or participate sufficiently and constructively, s/he will be dropped from the group and will be required to follow the "Enhanced Form" of the "Period Piece" paper. If a group as a whole seems to be dysfunctional, the group will be disbanded and each member will be required to follow the "Enhanced Form" of the "Period Piece" paper.

Adapted from: History of Economic Thought, ECN 615, Jerry Evensky, 1997.

EXAMPLE 6: THE "ONE PERSON'S VISION" PAPER

Objective

I believe that economics, indeed any field, evolves and that that evolution is driven by the nexus between the conditions in society and the people in the field. And as with the field as a whole, so too the individuals within the field evolve. Prior to their entry into the discourse of the field, individuals are nurtured by their personal experiences (e.g., cultural context or formal education) to see the world in certain ways. When they enter into the discourse of the field, each individual arrives to find a current "canon"—a shared vision and system of belief among those who make up the mainstream(s) leaders and participants in the field's discourse.

Based on her life experiences (which may or may not include learning the canon) an individual who wants to participate in the field forms her own vision and beliefs with respect to the field, and to the canon she finds upon her arrival. To the degree her vision and beliefs differ from that canon, she will act to influence the canon. Her vision continues to evolve as she lives a life in the field and beyond. At the same time, through her work and that of others in the field, the canon itself is evolving. Thus there is a nexus between the shaping of the individual and the shaping of the field; there is coevolution of individuals and canon. The most powerful participants are those who affect the canon most dramatically as it adapts to embody their vision (e.g., Marshall), or evolves as a reaction to their alternative vision (e.g., Marx), or does both (e.g., Keynes).

Your individual paper should analyze the intellectual development of an individual who has influenced or at least tried to influence economic thought: What was the nature of the effort and how did she come to make that contribution?

To accomplish this you should ask: What/who were the major influences on this person's development: family life as a child; teachers; professional experiences; social/political/economic norms, difficulties, or upheavals she endured; mentors, etc.? How did these influences manifest themselves in the intellectual development of this individual's vision? What is unique and creative about that vision, and how did the confluence of the influences you have identified allow this individual to go beyond the current discourse and create new ways of conceptualizing and organizing our understanding of the world?

Mechanics

The paper should written on a word processor. It should be approximately 20 pages (be sure to paginate your paper), double spaced, with 1" margins on the top and sides and 1.5" margins on the bottom. You should follow the format and citation style of the journal *History of Political Economy* (HB 1.H55 on the 4th floor of Bird Lib.)—see example below.

Notes on the "One Person's Vision" paper

1. You may not choose a person from the period covered by your group project, nor Adam Smith or Karl Marx or John Maynard Keynes.

2. All choices must be approved on or before Sept. 18.

3. Late papers will be penalized one letter grade per day, starting with the first deduction when the Economics Department office (110 Eggers) closes on the day the material is due and assessed one more grade penalty each successive day it is late when the office closes.

Adapted from: History of Economic Thought, ECN 615, Jerry Evensky, 1997.

12. EVALUATION

As well as being told about the purpose of course requirements, students should be told how their progress will be assessed, how their work will be evaluated, how grades will be assigned, and how you will use those grades to determine their final course grade. Your syllabus should include clear standards and criteria for any assessment strategies you will use.

Evaluation or assessment is a great deal more than giving a grade. The major part of evaluation, whether ongoing or final, should be in the form of comments on projects and papers, responses to student presentations, conversations, and other means of helping students to understand how they can do better.

Evaluation can be done by both instructors and students. It should include ongoing assessment procedures that allow students to learn to evaluate their own level of knowledge or skills. Ongoing assessment helps students to improve while the process is underway rather than being assessed when the course is over. For example, one instructor includes an example of a short essay question with annotated examples of inadequate, satisfactory, and excellent responses so that students may compare their own essays to the examples. You and your students should be aware of and use a variety of assessment procedures. Your syllabus can provide materials that will clarify the process for your students.

If your students will be writing papers, developing media productions, conducting research, or developing portfolios, they need to know what constitutes successful completion. If students will be taking exams, they should be told when the exams will be given, what material will be covered, what percentage of their final grade will be involved, if there will be a make-up exam, and what form the exam will take. Students usually want to know what types of questions will appear on a test (i.e., multiple choice, cases or problems, essay, etc.) as well as whether it is take-home, in-class, open- or closed-book.

Experimental activities including various laboratory sessions, internships, and fieldwork placements often involve different evaluation systems and personnel. It is important that both the student and the evaluator have a clear understanding of the criteria and methodology used.

EXAMPLE 1: ESSAY

Questions

Full essay questions allow you to expand upon issues, events, and larger questions. They provide you with an opportunity to set your answer in a broader historical context and to see the connection between events.

There are no "right" answers in history. Every answer is a different interpretation of events. Nonetheless, there are events and occurrences that are undeniably pertinent to certain questions. Your particular interpretation may influence what facts you include. Be sure to support your claims with examples from the readings or lectures!

In a full essay answer, we look for an introduction stating your approach to the question, a coherent argument supported by facts, and a short conclusion summarizing your findings in a sentence or two. Be clear and succinct in your answers. Do not write more than you need, but be wary of leaving out important details.

The following examples of essay answers should give you a good idea of what sort of information we are looking for. We have included an excellent, a satisfactory, and an unsatisfactory essay so that you can get an idea of what you should include in your own essays.

Adapted from: Eastern European History—From Independence to Independence: 1918 to the Present. Walter Ullmann and Jonathan P.G. Bach, 1993.

EXAMPLE 2: SENIOR THESIS/JURY PRESENTATIONS

The main objective of any presentation is clearly expressing the intended content matter. Presentation in design fields requires a combination of written, oral, and visual strategies. Both the oral presentation, which contains original visuals, and the thesis text, which explains the student's in-depth analysis and reasoning for the recommendations, are important and required. People may be stronger in one presentation mode than another. (Weaknesses in the oral presentation may be offset by excellence in graphics and by strength of the thesis document. It may be harder to compensate for weaknesses in the presentation of the thesis document, since the oral presentation will in all likelihood take place before the final draft of the thesis is finished.)

Presentations are evaluated based on the following criteria:

- Orderly format or structure
- Good verbal articulation

- Self-guiding text

- Visual display of information

- Appropriateness of the graphics

- Adequacy of the number of displays

- Clarity of delineation in graphics

Adapted from: Sancar, F. (1995) Senior thesis in Landscape Architecture. in Lunde, J.P. (Ed.). Reshaping Curricula: Revitalization Programs at Three Land Grant Universities. *Bolton, MA: Anker Publishing Company.*

EXAMPLE 3: SELF-EVALUATION

When one of the purposes of your course is that students learn to evaluate their own work, explanations of self-evaluation procedures should be included in your syllabus.

Congratulations! Even though you have finished the paper, you're not done yet! Before you mail in all of your informal writing, your drafts, and your final paper, we ask you to reflect and evaluate your work. But first, take a breather. Leave the paper alone for a while before doing the self-evaluation. It will help, when you write the self-evaluation, to have some distance from the paper. Give it a fresh read.

Next, we want you to evaluate what you've done from the perspective of two goals: your own and those of the course. From your own perspective, consider what you wanted to accomplish in doing the assignment. How were you looking to satisfy your own interests within the limits of the assignment itself? Evaluate the text accordingly. What disappoints you? What satisfies you? What do you have questions about? How would you approach it differently if you had to do it again? Now we want you to evaluate the paper from a teacher's perspective. What do you think your teacher will say when he or she reads the paper? If you find the teacher for this course too hard to imagine at this point, imagine a past teacher or someone you've respected. Finally, ask questions about things you're unsure about. Try to find patterns in these and note them specifically in your response.

If you need some help getting started, consider these five areas which your teacher will also be considering:

- How well does the text fulfill the assignment requirements in terms of subject matter and approach?

- Does the text present provocative ideas? Does the text make original conclusions or does it seem too obvious?

- Does the overall organization of the text work? Is there a discernible beginning, middle, and end? Do the ideas follow in the best order? Is there sufficient transition between one idea and the next? Can the reader always sense where s/he is at in the overall argument? Is all the material relevant?

- Is the purpose of each paragraph within the overall design clear? Does each paragraph have a discernible central focus? Is there a clear logic to the thinking in each paragraph?

- Is the style pleasing? Are sentences repetitious in structure? Does the prose sound too much like just a list?

Your self-evaluation need not be exhaustive. After reading your paper and considering it, focus on the areas that seem most relevant to your text. Please use specific examples from the text to support the claims you make about the paper. You may hand write your self-evaluation. It will probably be a couple of pages long.

We will read these self-evaluations *after* we read the papers and get a sense of them. The self-evaluations will be useful because we can compare what you've done in the paper with what you *think* you've done. This information helps your instructor respond to your work more effectively.

Adapted from: Writing Studio I. Course Guide. Nance Hahn, 1994.

EXAMPLE 4: LEARNING CONTRACT

Learning contracts provide a vehicle for making the planning of learning experiences a mutual undertaking between student and instructor. By participating in the process of diagnosing personal needs, deriving objectives, identifying resources, choosing strategies, and evaluating accomplishments, the student develops a sense of ownership of and commitment to the plan. Learning contracts make the learning objectives of any field or practical experience clear and explicit for both students and instructors. A brief outline of directions that you might give to students for developing learning contracts and one possible form for a contract are included here.

Objectives	Resource/ Strategies	Completion Date	Evidence	Verification

Learning Contracts

How do you develop a learning contract?

1. Diagnose your learning needs (what are the components for successful or outstanding performance in a particular field or activity?).

2. Specify your learning objectives (what you will learn).

3. Specify learning resources and strategies (how you will learn it).

4. Specify realistic target dates for completion.

5. Specify evidence of accomplishment (how you will show what you have learned).

6. Specify how the evidence will be validated.

7. Review your contract with consultants (peers, instructor, or other experts).

8. Carry out the contract (as you work, you may need to revise or renegotiate).

9. Evaluation of your learning (receiving some assurance that you have in fact learned what you set out to do).

Adapted with permission from Roger Hiemstra from materials he distributed in his classes. Original permission from Malcolm Knowles for his class materials.

EXAMPLE 5: PORTFOLIO

Because you are developing writers, the portfolio in this class will be both a display of mastery and evidence of development. When you read your work as a body, you can say more exactly how you've changed as a writer over the course of a semester, which of your abilities have been developed, where you've stretched your capabilities, and what things have been very professionally done. Reading your work as a body allows you to say with more confidence what your characteristic weaknesses and strengths are, and also what general qualities distinguish your "voice" (because your written voice is as distinctive in the words you use, as it is in the physical properties of your speech).

To underline your own learning and to show your development clearly to readers of your portfolio, we are going to ask you to write reflective statements that point out and account for the changes in your work over time. If you think of the portfolio as a museum showing of your work, the reflective statements will be our guide through the gallery. The opening reflective statement might be the talk that comes before the tour. This talk will explain the context and overall significance of the paintings on the walls. The prefaces are the brief comments that accompany individual pieces and direct the viewer's attention to points of interest. The prefaces help the reader appreciate the development and distinctiveness of the work. We will describe the reflective statements at greater length in the next section. First, let's get an idea of the overall shape of the portfolio.

The portfolio will be delivered in two parts. The first part is the portfolio proper, the selection of writing—your textual artifacts—that you choose to represent your work in the course, along with the reflective introduction that you write about that work. The second part is all of the remaining work you've done for the course (*all* the informal work and drafting). We need the remaining work to judge how you've chosen your work by looking at what you've left out.

Here are the contents of the portfolio proper:

- **Reflective Introduction (Item 1)**—This segment tells readers generally what they can expect with general reference to the contents of the portfolio. It gives readers some background and a preview of what they'll be looking at. It also includes a discussion of your current concerns as a writer and might suggest goals that you plan to work on next.

- **Special Exhibits (Item 2)**—These exhibits are brief (50 word) paragraphs that explain how you developed various pieces of writing and are attached to those pieces of writing.

- **Final Revisions of Papers and Prefaces to Polished Texts (Item 3)**—These papers are the final papers, "The Polished Work," from Modules 2 and 3 with brief (50 word) paragraphs attached that point out what changes or types of changes have been made.

- **Final Course Evaluation (Item 4)**—This final evaluation is the course evaluation form in the Coursepack. This form must be mailed in separately, to a separate address. Your instructor will not see the evaluation until s/he has assigned your course grade.

Adapted from: Writing Studio I. Course Guide. Nance Hahn, 1994.

EXAMPLE 6: LEARNING STYLE INVENTORY

While a formal self-evaluation is beyond the scope of this laboratory manual, we have included an informal learning style inventory to help you identify how you learn best.

How Do I Learn Best?

This test is to find out something about your preferred learning method. Research has been done on left brain-right brain differences in relation to personality differences, and studies show that individuals have preferred learning styles; i. e., some like to read while others would rather speak or listen. You will be asked 14 questions, and the answers you give will provide an indication of what your personal learning style may tend to be. Choose the answer that best explains your preference, and put the total of each letter in the boxes provided at the end of the test. Each letter presents a learning style that will be explained in the pages following the questions. The letter/style that receives the highest score may describe how you learn most effectively. Remember, there are no wrong or right answers, and none of the four styles is any better than the other. You may even find that there are two styles that receive approximately equal scores. This means that you may prefer to use a combination of those two learning methods.

Directions: Choose the answer that best explains your preference in each situation and put the letter in the box.

1. You are about to give directions to a person. She is staying in a hotel in town and wants to visit your house. She has a rental car. Would you:

    V) draw a map on paper
    A) tell her the directions
    R) write down the directions (without a map)
    K) pick her up from her hotel in your car

2. You are staying in a hotel and have a rental car. You would like to visit a friend whose address you do not know. Would you like him to:

V) draw you a map on paper
A) tell you the directions by phone
R) write down the directions (without a map)
K) pick you up from your hotel in your car

3. You have just received a copy of your itinerary for a world trip. This is of interest to a friend. Would you:
   V) show her on a map of the world
   A) call her immediately and tell her about it
   R) send her a copy of the printed itinerary

4. You are going to cook a dessert as a special treat for your family. Do you:
   V) thumb through the cookbook looking for ideas from the pictures
   A) ask others for advice
   R) refer to a specific cookbook where there is a recipe you know about
   K) cook something familiar without need for instructions

5. A group of tourists have been assigned to you to learn about national parks. Would you:
   V) show them slides and photographs
   A) give them a talk on national parks
   R) give them books on national parks
   K) drive them to a national park

6. You are about to purchase a new stereo. Other than price, what would most influence your decision?
   V) it looks really classy
   A) a friend talking about it
   R) reading details about it
   K) listening to it

7. Recall a time in your life when you learned how to do something like playing a new board game. (Try to avoid using a very physical skill like riding a bike.) How did you learn best?
   V) by using visual clues, like pictures or diagrams
   A) by listening to somebody explain it
   R) by reading written instructions
   K) by doing it

8. Which of these games do you prefer?
   V) Pictionary
   R) Scrabble
   K) Charades

9. You are about to learn to use a new program on a computer. Would you:
   A) call a friend and ask questions about it
   R) read the manual that comes with the program
   K) ask a friend to show you how to use it

10. You are not sure whether a word should be spelled dependent or dependant. Do you:
   V) see the word in your mind and choose the way it looks best
   A) sound it out in your mind
   R) look it up in the dictionary
   K) write both versions down

11. Apart from price, what would most influence your decision to buy a particular textbook?
   V) it looks OK
   A) a friend talking about it
   R) skimming through parts of it
   K) using a friend's copy

12. A new movie has arrived in town. What would most influence your decision to go/not to go?
   V) you saw a preview of it
   A) friends talked about it
   R) you read a review about it

13. What is your guess about how you learn best?
   V) visual cues
   A) listening and discussing
   R) reading
   K) doing, i.e., touch, taste, smell, feel

14. Do you prefer a professor who likes to use:
   V) flow diagrams, charts, slides
   A) discussion, guest speakers
   R) handouts, textbooks
   K) field trips, labs, practical sessions

Total of both pages   V   A   R   K
[V=visual, A=aural, R=read/write, K=kinesthetic]

Adapted from: Fleming, N. D., & Mills, C. (1992). Not another inventory, rather a catalyst for reflection. *To Improve the Academy, 11, 137–155.*

13. Grading Procedures

The following thoughts on grading are drawn from McKeachie (1994).

A student grade communicates to several groups—the student, parents, professors teaching advanced courses, graduate or professional school admission committees, prospective employers, etc. The person reading a grade typically wants some information about the student's recent performance that will predict the student's future abilities and performance.

- Students want to be able to use grades to assist them in decisions about what to major in, what other courses to take, and what possible careers to consider.

- Professors advising the student or determining admissions expect the grade to shed light on the student's motivation, skills, knowledge, ability, and work habits.

- Prospective employers use grades (along with interviews, letters of recommendation, and biographical data) to assist in decisions about how well the student will do in the job.

Grades serve a wide range of purposes, depending on who is reviewing them, but all of the uses are important and can affect major decisions about an individual. Ironically, while we place a great deal of faith in the capacity of grades to communicate effectively about student performance, most instructors feel uncomfortable with the process.

Davis (1993a) observes that how you grade depends a great deal on your values, assumptions, and educational philosophy. She suggests that if you develop clear guidelines from which to assess performance and grade carefully and consistently, you'll find grading processes more efficient and the essential function of grades—communicating students' level of mastery knowledge—will be easier.

Davis recommends several grading "do's":

- Communicate to students a clear rationale and policy on grading in your course syllabus.

- Grade on the basis of students' mastery of knowledge or skills.

- Avoid grading systems (such as grading on the curve) that put students in competition with their classmates, limiting the number of high grades. Healthy competition can be stimulated in other ways.

- Stress assessment of learning and progress toward goals; avoid overemphasis on grades.

- Keep students informed of their progress throughout the term so that students can maintain or improve performance; give a point total rather than a letter grade.

- Show the class's grade range and point distribution and what level is satisfactory.

- Provide enough opportunities for students to show what they know.

Two examples of grading procedure follow.

EXAMPLE 1: ABOUT GRADING

Grading in your WRT 115 course operates according to four simple principles:

1. The work in each of the four modules contributes one quarter (25%) to the final course grade.

2. Within each module the informal writing (including brainstorming, freewriting, coursepack exercises, field notes, plans, lists, paper drafts, etc.) counts as half (50%) of the module's work, and the module paper counts as half (50%).

3. Letter grades signify roughly the following about your performance:
   A = excellent; superior
   B = good
   C = average
   D = just passing
   F = unacceptable for course credit

Plus (+) and minus (-) are used for designations between categories. Thus a student could interpret a "B+" as "very good," a "C-" as "slightly below average," etc. (Syracuse University does not utilize the "A+," the "D+," or the "D-" grade.)

4. Grading is the province of the individual instructor. As in most college courses, the average student doing the average amount of work can expect to earn a grade of "C" for the course. However, students come into writing courses at all levels of proficiency; some may work very hard and still barely manage to bring their written products up to average college standards. Knowing as we do that a writing course is a course in language learning, and knowing as well that language learning proceeds most expeditiously under conditions of positive reinforcement, we reserve the right to adjust your earned grade half a grade (say from a "C+" to a "B-") in recognition of extraordinary effort and rapid development, as evidenced in both informal exercises and polished papers.

Adapted from: Writing Studio I. Course Guide. Nance Hahn, 1994.

EXAMPLE 2: GRADING CRITERIA

Grades for your performance and work will be based on the criteria outlined below. Any and/or all of these criteria will be applied to grading projects, depending on the objectives for the project.

Concept

Quality of idea: does it meet the objective of the communication?

Appropriateness: is idea relevant to objective of project?

Originality & Design

is it a unique approach or a rehash of ideas/techniques?

Composition/proportion: do elements work together with complementary sizes and arrangements?

Relationship of elements to the page: balance and harmony?

Color: do the elements combine to create the appropriate density/grey for the communication and page?

Surface: appropriate to the nature of the communication?

Information hierarchy: is it appropriate to the nature of the communication and information contained?

Format: appropriate to the nature of the communication/process

Idea development: has idea been developed to fullest extent?
Exploration: have all design options been explored, analyzed?
Refinement: has best idea and design been re-worked to perfection?
Risk-taking: have "rules" been challenged and successfully distorted or broken?

Execution

Technical skill: demonstrated mastery of tools and materials?
Attention to detail: are all facets of project complete?
Materials: appropriate choice of tools and materials used for execution of project?

Professionalism

Timeliness/ability to meet deadlines: attend to process of project regularly, and hand work in on time?
Following instructions: meet all criteria set up for project?
Neat/clean presentation: professional execution of work?
Integrity: work presented without compromise or excuses?

Attendance

Attend all classes.

3 absences = F grade (no excuses: if you are very ill or suffering from personal problems which prohibit you from attending class, please withdraw by the posted deadline). Even if you have legitimate excuses for being absent, it is just not feasible to assume that if you miss three or more classes you will be getting the information you need to earn 3 credits—especially since there is no textbook per se—only the software handouts, which are not a substitute for attending class at all. Be on time (for class and handing in assignments); being late (or coming unprepared) will count as an absence.

Participation

Ask questions, participate in critiques, assist peers, play with new information; challenge yourself.

Attitude

- Appreciation of and dedication to course objectives

- Demonstrate that the energy I put into teaching you something is well spent; learn and become proficient with the Mac. (That translates into work hard and earn an A, please.)

- Each assignment you turn in will be returned to you with a grading sheet. On it, you will find that several areas of your work have been reviewed and assigned a number grade. These numbers are added up and averaged to arrive at a grade for the entire project. Use the low numbers as an indication of areas where your skills are weak.

- The only way to earn an "INCOMPLETE" in this class is to be sick (and be able to prove it) on and off most of the semester. . . again, that's the policy of the University. I do not recommend incompletes as a viable alternative to withdrawing: this course requires too much one-on-one work to successfully work independently.

- I cannot make allowances for assignments which are handed in late—no excuses: your grade will drop 1.5 points (out of 4.0) for each class period that you are remiss in handing it in.

- I can, and I will, however, be delighted if you elect to redo any assignments for a better grade. Make sure that if you redo any project that you turn in the original assignment, and the original grading sheet along with the redone assignment so that I can grade the new one fairly. When you redo any project, the higher grade will be recorded, and the lower grade will be dropped.

- Late assignments may not be redone.

- Please be advised that redoing a project does not always ensure a better grade: Do your best the first time around and only redo assignments in dire cases.

Adapted from: Design Skills and Processes, CMD 282. Toni Toland, 1996.

14. How to Use the Syllabus

Students may not know how to use your syllabus effectively so include a brief explanation. You may find it useful to explain and go over the syllabus—to orient your students to its contents, form, and uses—during the first class meeting. Tell them that you will use the syllabus regularly throughout the course.

EXAMPLE 1: HOW TO USE THIS MANUAL

This student manual is designed to guide you through this course, Global Encounters. Independent study courses are special because you are not expected to meet the instructor face-to-face and talk to him/her during the course. So we have provided as much of that missing dialogue as possible.

The *Course Overview* describes the general scope of this course and what each of the main sections is about. It also explains exactly what is expected of you, how you are expected to read each section, and what the instructor expects you to look for in the course. *Tools for Independent Learning* is a quick review of different ways to study. Be sure to go through it carefully because it contains a variety of study skills and helpful hints for independent study courses like this one.

Next is the main text of the course. It is composed of five units, and each unit is further divided into lessons. The first unit is an introduction to the material in this course and the final lesson is a conclusion. Each requires a short writing assignment. The other four units have six lessons each. Every other lesson has a writing assignment in which you are asked to reflect on and compare the last two lessons.

Each lesson contains a number of instructive tools that we hope will help you in your study. The *Lesson Checklist* describes what is required of you in each lesson. The *Lesson Checklist* helps pace you and can be motivating because you can see what you have done and what you have not.

The text of the *Lesson* introduces you to the topic area. It will either tell you what is coming next or reflect on the last few sections. The text also models critical thinking, asking difficult questions about culture and people, a quality that is expected in your writing assignments.

Things to Think About as You Read is a list of questions to guide you and get you thinking about the implications of your reading. Answers to these questions help prepare you for the writing assignments.

Self-Tests and Answers are learning tools to help you get a sense of how well you understood a lesson and how much you need to review it. Self-tests assess your basic comprehension of a lesson with a few analytical questions too. These are not graded or sent to us but are for your use so you know how well you understood a section.

We hope that these sections are helpful in your study of Global Encounters: Comparing Western and Nonwestern Cultures.

Adapted from: Global Encounters: Comparing Western and Nonwestern Cultures. John Burdick, Yamuna Sangarasivam, and Tanya Cohen, 1994.

Example 2: Purpose of This Manual

This manual provides an outline of the basic structure of the course. Important information on matters such as the sequence of large group presentations, tests, and reading assignments is included along with specific exercises and information connected with the small section meetings of the course.

In the first part of this manual (the white pages), note that specific objectives for the various presentations and assignments for the entire course are spelled out for you. As you study for quizzes and exams, you should remember that questions will be based on these objectives. As you proceed through the course, you should have a clear idea about what you will be expected to know and do. You will also be able to determine how well you are doing as the course progresses.

In the latter part of this manual (the blue pages), you will find the material related to the small section part of the course. It is arranged in the form of a workbook and is intended to help you develop skills and knowledge related to the gathering and processing of information. These materials have been designed to assist you in dealing with specific assignments in CFS 101, but it is our intention that they should also prove useful in other courses; e.g., the material on the library and the individual and group assignments should give you a head start in dealing with future assignments in many of your courses. The materials included in the white and blue sections are designed to complement one another and help you to accomplish the objectives of the course in an enjoyable and rewarding manner.

Adapted from: Human Ecology, CFS 101, College For Human Development. Syracuse University: Center for Instructional Development, Pickett, R. (Ed.), 1993.

15. How to Study for This Course

Different courses require different study patterns and practices. Include in your syllabus the strategies that you have found to work for other students in your course.

EXAMPLE: HOW TO STUDY FOR THIS COURSE

You will be studying the material for this course independently, and we have designed this *Student Manual* to provide you with information necessary for your success. Each unit contains a short background essay to familiarize you with the material and to help you focus on what is important. The background essay is not a substitute for the assigned reading—both are essential for successful completion of the course. When you begin to read the required texts, you will encounter many details such as economic figures, voting records, and other statistics. Do not worry; you are not required to know all of the figures in these books. Below is a list of the kinds of information you should pay attention to. This is the type of information that will appear in the exam questions.

General Discernible Trends

These include such trends as: problems with ethnic minorities; shifts from one type of government to another (e.g., democratic to authoritarian); the steady influence of one country in another; and rising political instability accompanying economic failure.

Names of the Most Prominent Actors

This includes almost all heads of state (usually kings, presidents, and prime ministers) and often important military leaders, politicians, and dissidents. It should be clear from the reading which actors are most important. There will also be clues in the background essays and the unit questions (see below).

Crucial Dates

The beginnings and ends of wars and the formation (or dissolution) of countries are key dates. Also important are major uprisings (e.g., Hungary 1956), invasions (e.g., Czechoslovakia 1968), ascents to power (e.g., Gorbachev), coups (e.g., Pilsudski, 1926), treaties (e.g., Trianon, 1920), and economic disasters (e.g., the Depression, 1929). It may be useful to create a timeline for yourself as you read through the material. Be aware of overall context while you keep track of important dates.

You should review the Unit Objectives, the Key Terms, and the Unit Background sections in the *Student Manual* before you begin each corresponding reading assignment. Each unit will also contain study questions, which should be answered after you finish the reading assignments. You may even wish to review the Study Questions before you do the readings so you have an idea of what to look for as you read. If you know someone else involved in this course, you may wish to discuss the material and the answers to the questions together.

Adapted from: Eastern European History—From Independence to Independence: 1918 to the Present. Walter Ullmann and Jonathan P.G. Bach, 1993.

16. Content Information

This section may include any of a wide variety of materials. In it you can provide students with information specific to selected units and topics or reference material to be used throughout the course such as a glossary of relevant terms or a chronology of important events. Supplementary information such as reprints of complicated diagrams or data used in class in a problem solving exercise may be included in the manual, as worksheet or organizer for student note taking. A bibliography helps students to find further readings on a topic.

While most students are familiar with library research, it may be useful to acquaint them with the logistics of your library, the use of certain periodical indices, or other sources specific to your content area.

EXAMPLE: CONTENT INFORMATION

A Note on Terminology

In this course, "Eastern Europe" refers to the countries of Poland, former Czechoslovakia (presently the Czech Republic and Slovakia), the former German Democratic Republic (East Germany), Hungary, Romania, Bulgaria, Albania, and the former Yugoslavia (presently the independent states of Slovenia, Croatia, Bosnia-Hercegovina, Macedonia, and Yugoslavia, which now consists only of Serbia and Montenegro). The "Balkans" refers only to the states of former Yugoslavia, Romania, Bulgaria, Albania, and Greece, a country which only figures nominally in our course.

Adapted from: Eastern European History—From Independence to Independence: 1918 to the Present. Walter Ullmann and Jonathan P.G. Bach, 1993.

17. LEARNING TOOLS

This section on learning tools may be more comprehensive than many people want to include in a syllabus. Those who want something more concise may summarize these materials.

You, the student, are the center of the learning process. While your teacher can provide you with the guidance and materials that you need to succeed, it is your responsibility to set goals, plan your work, make notes from readings, lectures and discussions, and schedule the time you will need to complete assignments.

Developing good study skills can not only save you time and energy, but can also help you learn better, independently, and with less guesswork.

This section covers five effective study skills that will promote learning.

- Self-management
- Making notes
- Reading to learn
- Studying with others
- Taking tests

SELF-MANAGEMENT

Review the course syllabus and other course materials. Then consider what *you* want to accomplish in the course and what it will take to accomplish it. Once you have set attainable goals for yourself, plot out how to achieve them. Ask yourself, "What must I do to complete the course successfully? How much effort am I willing to put into the course? How can I make the best use of my time? What part of the day/week is best for me to study?" Also consider where you will study. Using an area that is free from distractions will increase your efficiency.

Consider how you will manage your time wisely. It is helpful to organize a schedule, marking key dates on a weekly/monthly calendar. Schedule times for reading, making useful notes, working on projects, reviewing material, and studying for tests. You may need to renegotiate your schedule if certain activities take more or less time than you had anticipated.

Try to pace your work load evenly. Consider breaking large assignments into smaller segments. For example, if a course has several assignments that consist of several chapters or modules, don't try to do all the work in one session. Instead, break down the units into more manageable, readily digestible subunits. For longer papers (or other special projects) plan time to write first drafts, revisions, and final versions.

Part of any good plan also includes a reward system. When you achieve a goal, reward yourself. Do something you would like to do. Include incentives when planning your course workload.

Self-Management Techniques Include the Following:

- Set learning goals.

- Plan and organize a schedule with ample time for reading, studying, reviewing, and studying for tests.

- Adjust your schedule as the course progresses.

- Break down work into manageable units.

- Pace the course workload evenly.

- Use a study location free of distractions.

- Review periodically.

- Set incentives or rewards for the completion of a section.

READING TO LEARN

Reading to learn is a specialized form of reading that requires more effort than most other forms. Using the steps that follow will improve your understanding of the material you read.

Read with a Purpose

Determine the purpose of your reading. Are you reading for the general idea, for the structure of an argument, for close scrutiny of detail, inference, and application? Adjust your speed and process accordingly.

Scan the Text

Textbooks are divided and subdivided into units and chapters, each with their own titles and headings. First, read the introduction to the text and any summaries. Surveying the structure of the text will help you understand and organize the concepts you will be reading. This process also works for reading other types of course material.

Preview for the General Idea

Preview the chapter to get a general idea of the material. Look at the headings, photos, maps, and tables. Before you begin to read the material, look over the glossary or key terms for new and already familiar concepts.

Question the Text

Formulate *questions* about the text by changing each heading or title into a question. The headings should reflect the main ideas of the text. When you have completed a section, see if you can answer the questions. What new questions were raised?

First Reading

Read the text, concentrating on the major ideas. You may want to underline or highlight them. At this point, however, focus on the major ideas, not the details.

Reread to Check Understanding

At the end of each section, *summarize* the main ideas, then *restate* the concepts in your own words. If you are confused, go back and reread the part you don't fully understand. When you have finished reading, go back and make notes, margin notes, or underline key phrases in the book.

Other techniques that some students find useful are to visualize the information as you read it, relate it to something you already know, read out loud or think aloud, and discuss the reading with someone else.

Review

Review the information in the text by rereading your notes, questions, and any exercises that have been assigned. Some other review techniques are to use index cards to review key terms, recite the information out loud, and explain the information to someone else.

Reading Techniques Include the Following:

- Determine your purpose for reading.

- Preview the text (titles, maps, photos, summaries, intro).

- Read for main ideas.

- Turn titles and headings into questions.

- Summarize in your own words.

- Reread, visualize, relate, think aloud.

- Review.

MAKING USEFUL NOTES

Making useful notes from readings and lectures is an important study skill that can help you learn and review information. A key word here is *useful.* Useful notes are those that are not only correct and accurate, but also help you to study for your course. A second key is the emphasis on *making* rather than taking notes. Your notes, written in your own words, should reflect your decisions about what is important to know in course readings, lectures, labs, and discussions. To make your notes useful for learning, try the following:

Prior to class: Complete assigned readings and make an organized set of notes. Include any questions raised by the readings.

During class: Lectures generally blend your instructors' insights with materials from the readings. If you have completed the readings and written an organized set of notes, you should be able to take notes from the lecture selectively.

After class: Rewrite notes to include new insights and questions raised.

Periodically: Review and rewrite notes to clarify issues.

Summarizing

After reading a section, it is helpful to summarize what you have just read in your own words. The act of writing this information helps you to remember it. Of course, the notes will be valuable later in reviewing for tests. Aside from writing paraphrased notes, you can also create graphic organizers like outlines, flowcharts, and trees.

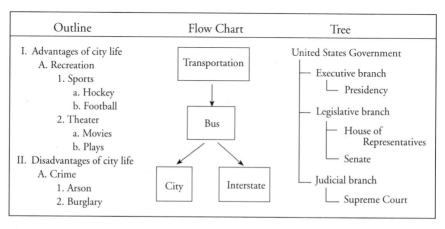

Concept Maps

Another method of making notes is connecting the different ideas into what is called a *concept map*. Start by placing the central idea in the middle of a piece of paper. Add related ideas and draw lines to them from the central idea. Each idea can be further subdivided. The lines represent the relationship between and among each of the ideas, so you can draw any number of lines and the map can have any shape.

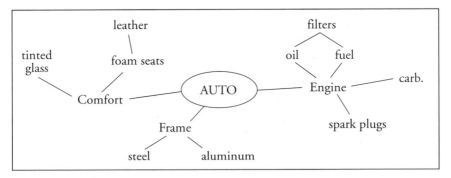

Underlining

In the section on reading a text, it was suggested that you underline the main ideas. It is not the actual underlining of the text that helps you learn, but the process of deciding which information is worth underlining. Avoid the common pitfall of underlining everything and anything. Be selective and underline only relevant information in short segments.

Making Useful Notes Includes the Following Techniques:

- Identify main ideas.
- Summarize ideas or text.
- Create outlines, flowcharts, trees, concept maps.
- Underline selectively.
- Rewrite notes.

STUDYING WITH OTHERS

One of the best ways of learning is to study with someone else. Get to know one or more students enrolled in this course and work together. After a reading assignment, review the answers to any questions you have been given and discuss what you believe were the major points. Test each other on specific knowledge. If practice test items are available, go over them together before taking an exam. If not, formulate possible test questions, practice writing answers, and review them together.

Or try explaining what you are trying to learn to a friend who has never studied the subject. Your understanding of the material is clarified when you must present ideas so that others can understand them. Studying with others has been shown to be one of the most effective ways to study and learn.

EXAMINATIONS AND TESTS

Tests are designed to see how well you have learned. Try the following steps to improve your test-taking skills.

Before the Test

Reread the materials that will be covered on the test and ask yourself what the important points are.

- Look for the points emphasized in your syllabus.

- An "open book" test doesn't mean that you can disregard the reading. In an open-book test, the instructor is looking for how well you can demonstrate your understanding of the concepts. The exam will focus on how you support your position.

- Don't study differently for an objective test than you would for an essay test. Both formats incorporate the use of broad concepts as well as specific points.

- Try outlining the main points in your readings. It is often helpful to write out an answer to an essay question you think may be asked. Wait a day or two and then look at your answer to see if you are satisfied with it.

Review for a Test by Using the Following Techniques:

- Guess at possible questions and answer them.

- Compare the course outline with your syllabus and your reading. Whenever you find a subject that appears on all three, you know you have located an important issue and should look it over again.

- Review key terms from chapters and lectures.

- If you are working with formulas or operations, practice them several times.

- If possible, work with someone else who is taking the same course and go over major concepts with them.

Taking the Test or Exam

Regardless of whether you will be taking an objective test or an essay test, follow these procedures:

- Get a good night's sleep before the test.

- Have at least two pens or pencils ready for the test.

- Try not to be nervous. *RELAX.*

- When you get the test, *read the directions* carefully.

- Read quickly through the test to get an idea of what kinds of questions are included.

- Number all your answers clearly, and write your name on each page.

- Make sure you follow directions. If you are asked to choose between several essay questions, take the time to select those that you are most prepared for and are interested in.

These learning tools have been adapted from those used for Syracuse University Independent Study Courses. Syracuse University: Center for Instructional Development.

CHECKLIST

This guide has been designed to help you in developing a learning-centered course syllabus that will fit the conditions in which you and your students work. What you include in your syllabus will be determined by the needs of your students, the type of course you are offering, and the rationale underlying your course. The checklist below can serve as a guide when you prepare your syllabus.

	1. TITLE PAGE
	2. TABLE OF CONTENTS
	3. INSTRUCTOR INFORMATION
	4. LETTER TO THE STUDENT
	5. PURPOSE OF THE COURSE
	6. COURSE DESCRIPTION
	7. COURSE AND UNIT OBJECTIVES
	8. RESOURCES
	9. READINGS
	10. COURSE CALENDAR
	11. COURSE REQUIREMENTS
	12. EVALUATION
	13. GRADING PROCEDURES
	14. HOW TO USE THE SYLLABUS
	15. HOW TO STUDY FOR THIS COURSE
	16. CONTENT INFORMATION
	17. LEARNING TOOLS

Part III
Resources

This final part of the book provides two types of resources. The first, in Suggested Readings, are published materials that focus on specific aspects of students and learning, and they are organized by subject matter. These readings provide a sound foundation for thinking about what a learning-centered syllabus is and what it might include.

The second, in References, are sources that have been used in this guide. These, too, may help in your exploration and creation of a learning-centered syllabus.

SUGGESTED READINGS

This bibliography has been arranged in the following categories: general teaching, active learning, assessment, computer technology, cooperative learning, course and curriculum design, critical thinking, and student differences. It also includes some references on developing an annotated teaching portfolio to document your innovations and improvements in teaching.

GENERAL TEACHING

The following books provide tested strategies, tips, and advice for both new and more experienced college teachers.

Barr, R. B., & Tagg, J. (1995). From teaching to learning: A new paradigm for undergraduate education. *Change 27,* 6.

Boice, R. (1996). *First-order principles for college teachers: Ten basic ways to improve the teaching process.* Bolton, MA: Anker.

Davis, B. G. (1993). *Tools for teaching.* San Francisco, CA: Jossey-Bass.

Davis, J. R. (1993). *Better teaching, more learning: Strategies for success in postsecondary settings.* Phoenix, AZ: Oryx.

Hatfield, S. R. (Ed.). (1995). *The seven principles in action: Improving undergraduate education.* Bolton, MA: Anker.

McKeachie, W. J. (1994). *Teaching tips: Strategies, research, and theory for college and university teachers.* 9th edition. Lexington, MA: D. C. Heath.

Roth, J. K. (Ed.). (1997). *Inspiring teaching: Carnegie professors of the year speak.* Bolton, MA: Anker.

Seldin, P., & Associates. (1995). *Improving college teaching.* Bolton, MA: Anker.

Wright, W. A., & Associates. (1995). *Teaching improvement practices: Successful strategies for higher education.* Bolton, MA: Anker.

ACTIVE LEARNING

Meyers, C., & Thomas, T. (1993). *Promoting active learning: Strategies for the college classroom.* San Francisco, CA: Jossey-Bass.

This book is a practical guide to successful strategies for active learning, in which students talk and listen, read, write, and reflect as they become directly involved in the instructional process. The authors present a wide range of teaching tools including problem solving exercises, student projects, informal group work, simulations, case studies, role-playing.

ASSESSMENT

Angelo, T. A., & Cross, K. P. (1993). *Classroom assessment techniques: A handbook for college teachers.* San Francisco, CA: Jossey-Bass.

This book offers teachers detailed, how-to advice on classroom assessment, estimating the ease of use, providing concise descriptions and step-by-step procedures for planning and implementing fifty assessment techniques. It includes a Teaching Goals Inventory for identifying and clarifying instructional goals, which is cross-indexed to help locate appropriate techniques. (See also Wlodkowski, 1995 under Student Differences, this section.)

COMPUTER TECHNOLOGY

If you are seeking information on computer technology, the *Chronicle of Higher Education* has a regular feature that highlights new software developed by faculty and commercial venders.

Copyright regulations also apply to software; unauthorized copying is illegal. EDUCOM, a consortium of higher education institutions interested in integrating information technology into classrooms, curriculum, and research can provide a brochure that describes guidelines for fair, ethical and legal use of licensed and unlicensed software (bitnet: PUBS@ EDUCOM.BITNET; Internet: PUBS@EDUCOM.EDU). *Questions and answers on copyright for the campus community.* (1989). New York, NY: The National Association of College Stores and The Association of American Publishers. Or try: www.copyright.com

COOPERATIVE LEARNING

Johnson, D.W., Johnson, R. T., & Smith, K. A. (1991). *Cooperative learning: Increasing college faculty instructional productivity. ASHE-ERIC Higher Education Report No. 4.* Washington, DC: The George Washington University, School of Education and Human Development.

Cooperative learning is the instructional use of small groups in which students work together to maximize their own and each others' learning. The conceptual approach to cooperative learning described in this monograph is based on research on general principles of how to structure cooperative learning activities for a teacher's specific subject area, curriculum, students, and setting. The authors propose that to be cooperative, five components must be present: 1) a group must have clear positive interdependence; 2) members must promote each others' learning and success face-to-face; 3) members must hold each other personally and individually accountable to do his or her fair share of the work; 4) groups must use appropriately the interpersonal and small-group skills needed for cooperative groups to be successful; 5) a group should process how effectively members are working together.

COURSE AND CURRICULUM DESIGN

Diamond, R. M. (1989). *Designing and improving courses and curricula in higher education.* San Francisco, CA: Jossey-Bass.

The author offers guidelines for every phase of designing and planning a curriculum: analyzing and improving existing programs as well as developing, implementing, and evaluating new ones. Detailed case studies are included.

Gardiner, L. F. (1994). *Redesigning higher education: Producing dramatic gains in student learning. ASHE-ERIC Higher Education Report No. 7.* Washington, DC: The George Washington University, Graduate School of Education and Human Development.

The author examines a growing body of knowledge about student learning, college outcomes, and the effectiveness of various options for instruction and assessment to identify a set of practices that will lead to better learning for students.

Jenrette, M. S., & Napoli, V. (1994). *The teaching/learning enterprise: Miami-Date Community College's blueprint for change.* Bolton, MA: Anker.

The authors describe the overhaul of the college's philosophy and practices during the Miami-Dade Community College Teaching/Learning Project.

Lunde, J. P. (Ed.). (1995). *Reshaping curricula: Revitalization programs at three land grant universities.* Bolton, MA: Anker.

The 25 essays reveal how professors in each of three major state universities revitalized their curricula.

CRITICAL THINKING/WRITING

Bean, J. C. (1996). *Engaging ideas: The professor's guide to integrating writing, critical thinking, and active learning in the classroom.* San Francisco, CA: Jossey-Bass.

The author integrates writing with other critical thinking activities, presenting a wide variety of strategies for stimulating active learning. The book offers concrete advice on how to design courses, structure assignments, use class time, critique student performance, and to model critical thinking themselves.

Kurfiss, J. G. (1988) *Critical thinking: Theory, research, practice and possibilities. ASHE-ERIC Higher Education Report No. 2.* Washington, DC: Association for the Study of Higher Education.

The report is concerned with the formal development of critical thinking in higher education. Most colleges and universities aspire to produce graduates who can make judgments in complex situations on the basis of sound reason, adequate evidence, and articulated values. It surveys theory, research, teaching practice, and institutional programs in addressing several questions: What is critical thinking? How does it develop? What role does knowledge play in critical thinking? Do educational practices affect the ability to think critically? The report examines critical thinking on three levels: argument skills, cognitive processes, intellectual processes. The author provides numerous examples of programs and courses that successfully integrate critical thinking with content learning suggestions on how to incorporate thinking into the curriculum.

STUDENT DIFFERENCES

Social and cultural differences can affect student expectations of a college education: in differences in the way they take in, process, construct, and make meaningful connections with new knowledge; in their preparation for academic study; and in their needs and desires for support and challenge.

The following sources will help you to understand the broad patterns of student learning and development that influence students' responses to learning situations. They will also help you to guide your students as they struggle to understand their own particular evolving pattern. (See also Bean, 1996; Kurfiss, 1988; and Davis, 1983 in this section.)

Belenky, M. F., Clinchy, B. M., Goldberger, N. R., & Tarule, J. M. (1986). *Women's ways of knowing: The development of self, voice, and mind.* New York, NY: Basic Books.

Perry, W. G., Jr. (1970). *Forms of intellectual and ethical development in the college years.* New York, NY: Holt, Rinehart, & Winston.

These two classics in the field are illuminating and helpful explanations of positions or perspectives of intellectual and ethical development in student thinking. Perry's study is limited to a focus on white males. Belenky and her colleagues argue that women have developed along different intellectual lines from men due to different value orientations.

Ericksen, S. C., & Strommer, D. W. (1991). *Teaching college freshman.* San Francisco, CA: Jossey-Bass.

Drawing on freshman learning research, the authors offer practical guidance on how to teach and provide academic support for students in their crucial first year. They examine issues such as students' diverse educational backgrounds, learning styles, expectations about learning, and their educational goals and values. They identify common anxieties, habits, and assumptions that can impede learning progress, and they present strategies for overcoming these obstacles.

Gardner, H. (1993). *Multiple intelligences: The theory in practice.* New York, NY: Basic Books.

Many instructors have found Gardner's analysis helpful when planning their teaching/learning environment. Gardner defines intelligence as the ability to solve problems or to fashion products that are valued in one or more cultural or community settings and proposes that human beings are capable of knowing the world in at least seven different ways— through language, logical-mathematical analysis, spatial representation, musical thinking, the use of the body to solve problems or to make things, an understanding of other individuals, and understanding ourselves. People differ in the relative strength and dominance of these intelligences—and in the ways these intelligences are invoked and combined. Gardner proposes that any concept worth teaching can be approached from at least five different entry points: narration, logical-quantitative, foundational, esthetic, and experiential. The teacher makes available several entry points at the beginning or over time so that there is a good chance that students with differing intelligence profiles will find relevant and engaging ways of learning.

Friedman, E. G., Kolmar, W. K., Flint, C. B., & Rothenberg, P. (Eds.). (1996). *Creating an inclusive classroom: A teaching sourcebook from The New Jersey Project.* New York, NY: Teachers College Press.

This volume gathers over 40 innovative syllabi, teaching resources, and reflective essays intended to move college curriculum toward one that is inclusive, nonsexist, nonracist, and multicultural.

Kolb, D. A. (1985). *Learning style inventory.* Boston, MA: McBer.

The author identifies a learning cycle grounded in an experiential model of learning. The four phases of the cycle—concrete experience, reflective observation, abstract conceptualization, and active experimentation—each require a different process to acquire different information and to learn different skills.

Wlodkowski, R. J., & Ginsberg, M. B. (1995). *Diversity and motivation: Culturally responsive teaching.* San Francisco, CA: Jossey-Bass.

This volume offers real world guidance and suggestions for respectful teaching practices that cross disciplines and cultures. Using a motivational framework for culturally responsive teaching applied in a postsecondary setting, the authors describe learning strategies and structures necessary to establish inclusion, enhance meaning, and engender competence. Included is a syllabus and an analysis of it that shows where the syllabus is consistent with norms, procedures, and structures of culturally responsive teaching and where improvement from this perspective is possible.

TEACHING PORTFOLIOS

Your learning-centered syllabus can serve as a significant document in your professional portfolio as evidence of innovation and significant improvement in the quality of your teaching. The following provide useful information on teaching portfolios.

Seldin, P. (1997). *The teaching portfolio: A practical guide to improved performance and promotion/tenure decisions.* 2nd edition. Bolton, MA: Anker.

Seldin, P., & Associates (1993). *Successful use of teaching portfolios.* Bolton, MA: Anker.

Zubizarreta, J. (1995). Using teaching portfolio strategies to improve course instruction. In P. Seldin & Associates (Eds.), *Improving college teaching.* Bolton, MA: Anker.

REFERENCES

American Library Association. (1989). *Final report on information literacy.* Washington, DC: American Library Association.

Angelo, T. A., & Cross, K. P. (1993). *Classroom assessment techniques: A handbook for college teachers.* San Francisco, CA: Jossey-Bass.

APA. (1994). *Publication manual of the American Psychological Association,* 4th edition. Washington, DC: American Psychological Association.

Barr, R. B., & Tagg, J. (1995). From teaching to learning: A new paradigm for undergraduate education. *Change, 27,* 6, 12-25.

Bean, J. C. (1996). *Engaging ideas: The professor's guide to integrating writing, critical thinking, and active learning in the classroom.* San Francisco, CA: Jossey-Bass.

Bergquist, W., & Sharpe, D. (1996). *Feast: Curricular abundance in a time of scarcity.* Point Arena, CA: Magnusson Press.

Brown, A. L., Ash, D., Rutherford, M., Nakagawa, K., Gordon, A., & Campione, J. C. (1993). Distributed expertise in the classroom. In G. Salomon (Ed.), *Distributed cognitions: Psychological and educational considerations.* Cambridge, England: Cambridge University Press.

Burdick, J., Sangarasivam, Y., & Cohen, T. (1994). *Global encounters: Comparing Western and Nonwestern cultures.* In A. O. Roberts (Ed.), Syracuse, NY: Syracuse University Center for Instructional Development.

Davis, B. G. (1993a). *Tools for teaching.* San Francisco, CA: Jossey-Bass.

Davis, J. R. (1993b). *Better teaching, more learning: Strategies for success in postsecondary settings.* Phoenix, AZ: Oryx.

Diamond, R. M. (1989). *Designing and improving courses and curricula in higher education.* San Francisco, CA: Jossey-Bass.

Evensky, J. (1997). *History of Economic Thought, ECN 615.* Syracuse, NY: Syracuse University Center for Instructional Development.

Evensky, J. (1997). *Understanding Rosie the Riveter: Research seminar on values and choices, ECN 204.* Syracuse, NY: Syracuse University Center for Instructional Development.

Fleming, N. D., & Mills, C. (1992). Not another inventory, rather a catalyst for reflection. *To Improve the Academy, 11,* 137-155.

Gardiner, L. F. (1994). *Redesigning higher education: Producing dramatic gains in student learning. ASHE-ERIC Higher Education Report No. 7.* Washington, DC: The George Washington University, Graduate School of Education and Human Development.

Gardner, H. (1993). *Multiple intelligences: The theory in practice.* New York, NY: Basic Books.

Hahn, N. (1994). *Writing Studio I. Course guide.* Syracuse, NY: Syracuse University Center for Instructional Development.

Hiemstra, R. (1994) distributed course materials.

Ismail, B., & Slocum, D. (1993). *Financial accounting systems. Student manual.* In A. O. Roberts (Ed.), Syracuse, NY: Syracuse University Center for Instructional Development.

Johnson, D.W., Johnson, R. T., & Smith, K. A. (1991). *Cooperative learning: Increasing college faculty instructional productivity. ASHE-ERIC Higher Education Report No. 4.* Washington, DC: The George Washington University, School of Education and Human Development.

Kurfiss, J. G. (1988) *Critical thinking: Theory, research, practice and possibilities. ASHE-ERIC Higher Education Report No. 2.* Washington, DC: Association for the Study of Higher Education.

Lough, J. R. (1997). The Carnegie Professors of the Year: Models for teaching success. In J. Roth (Ed.), *Inspiring teaching: Carnegie Professors of the Year speak.* Bolton, MA: Anker.

McKeachie, W. C. (1994). *Teaching tips: Strategies, research, and theory for college and university teachers,* 9th edition. Lexington, MA: D. C. Heath.

Meyers, C., & Thomas, T. (1993) *Promoting active learning: Strategies for the college classroom.* San Francisco, CA: Jossey-Bass.

Pascarella, E., & Terenzini, P. (1991). *How college affects students: Findings and insights from twenty years of research.* San Francisco, CA: Jossey-Bass.

Pickett, R. (Ed.). *Human Ecology, CFS 101, College for Human Development.* Syracuse, NY: Syracuse University Center for Instructional Development.

Polyson, S., Saltzberg, S., & Godwin-Jones, R. (1996, September). A practical guide to teaching with the world-wide web. *Syllabus,* 12-16.

Project Advance. (1995). *Planning your course resource manual.* Prepared for instructors of *Writing Studio 105.* Syracuse, NY: Syracuse University Center for Instructional Development.

Sancar, F. (1995). Senior thesis in landscape architecture. In J. P. Lunde (Ed.), *Reshaping curricula: Revitalization programs at three land grant universities.* Bolton, MA: Anker.

Shulman, L., & Hutchings, P. (1994). Excerpt from Peer Review of Teaching Workshop sponsored by AAHE.

Simmons, S.R. (1995). Using decision cases in a capstone course. In J. P. Lunde (Ed.), *Reshaping curricula: Revitalization programs at three land grant universities.* Bolton, MA: Anker.

Thau, S. (1992). *Ethics: Theories and controversies.* A Syracuse University Independent Study Course. Syracuse, NY: Syracuse University Center for Instructional Development.

Toland, T. (1996). *Design skills and processes, CMD 282.* Syracuse, NY: Syracuse University Center for Instructional Development.

Ullman, W., & Bach, J. P. G. (1993). *Eastern European history—from independence to independence: 1918 to the present.* In A. O. Roberts (Ed.), Syracuse, NY: Syracuse University Center for Instructional Development.

Wallin, T. O. (1994). *Perspectives of business and management, SOM 122: The management freshman gateway course. Course handbook.* Syracuse, NY: Syracuse University Center for Instructional Development.

Wlodkowski, R. J., & Ginsberg, M. B. (1995). *Diversity and motivation: Culturally responsive teaching.* San Francisco, CA: Jossey-Bass.

Index

DATE DUE

JUN 3 0 2009			